MW01243762

Experience Supernatural Change

TRANSFORMATION
workbook

Kent & Beverly Mattox

Transformation Workbook: Experience Supernatural Change

ISBN = black and white = 9798839897304

Note this is the black and white edition of color book = 9798839891319

Copyright 2022 Kent and Beverly Mattox, All rights reserved.

For more information, contact:
Word Alive, 122 Allendale Rd, Oxford, AL 36203, 256- 831-5280

Cited Scriptures noted in the following abbreviations come from:

AMP— Amplified Bible
KJV— King James Version
MSG— the Message
NASB— New American Standard Bible
NIV— New International Version
NKJV— New King James Version
NLT— New Living Translation
MSG— the Message

Access book resources at
TransformationBook.online

TABLE OF CONTENTS

INTRODUCTION

We've been in ministry for several decades. We've traveled overseas and shared the Gospel in third world countries. We've attended large crusades and revivals.

And we've served in the same church— a unique expression of the Body of Christ— for 20+ years.

We've been around "the Church" a lot. A whole lot.

A few things have perplexed us, though:

- If Jesus said we would do greater works than He did, where is the power (John 14:12)?

- If Jesus said He didn't intend to take us out of the world but to leave us in the world— even though we're not "of" the world— then why do Christians so often feel the need to withdraw (John 17:11,14-15)?

- If Jesus said the gates of hades will not prevail against His Church, His *ekklesia*, then why do we so often feel defeated (Matthew 16:18)?

- If the first generation of disciples post-resurrection actually "turned the world upside down" (read: back to "right side up"), then why don't we see the same power and presence today?

This workbook is our attempt to wrestle with— and provide a path forward through— those questions. More importantly, **this manual provides you with a tool to "live out" your faith with power, amidst the people you know, in such a way that you don't feel defeated but— rather — see God's power and presence manifest in your life (and in theirs).**

We pulled together our thoughts, concepts the Lord revealed to us in prayer, and ideas we learned from other followers of Christ— faithful men and women who struggled in their own way with the same questions we had. Then, we created a notebook (an actual three ring binder) and invited a handful of couples to our home.

Together, we ate and laughed and prayed and talked through the transformation pathway with them over the course of four weeks. And, our goal was simple:

- Understand in its purest form what our "commission" as Christians is (all based on those questions above, oddly enough)

- Discover how to not only know that commission, but also do it in our daily lives (not just on Sundays while we gather in a building)

- Have fun and enjoy true community with each other in the process

We believe you can do the same, which is why we've made this resource available to you.

Consider this manual your guidebook. Over the next four lessons you'll engage with four concepts (these are, you'll notice, the titles and main ideas for each chapter in the book):

1. **Identity**: My uniqueness is a gift from God Himself. I matter because of who I am, more so than anything I do. The impact I make on the world is an overflow of who I am.

2. **Alignment**: The second step in my transformation is to move into alignment with the Kingdom of God, specifically by leveraging our two most important resources: time and money.

3. **Empowerment**: I take the values of the Kingdom with me everywhere I go. The church isn't a place; the church is a people. We don't "go to" church; we "go as" the church.

4. **Assignment**: The church exists wherever the people of God go. As such, we take the message of the Kingdom with us. Our assignment is to bless the people we encounter, leaning deeper into the divine connections.

THE PATH

IDENTITY	ALIGNMENT	EMPOWERMENT	ASSIGNMENT
DISCOVER WHO GOD UNIQUELY MADE ME TO BE	*REORDER MY MOST VALUABLE ASSETS*	*TAKE THE PRESENCE WITH ME IN EVERY AREA OF LIFE*	*BLESS THE PEOPLE GOD PLACES BEFORE ME*

This manual, though it works "on its own" as you study and apply the concepts, was created for us in the context of community— a small group. I encourage you to work through this material with others.

For each lesson, consider the following:

- Read the material before your group meets— and even review the questions in the "Transform" section at the end of each chapter.

- Watch the bonus videos (you have free access), and work through the questions.

- Attend your group ready to share— to be challenged and to grow (together) as you do.

Thank you for joining us on this journey. I believe the material you hold in your hand will empower you to experience change as well as become an agent of change in the world around you.

VISIT THE TRANSFORMATION WEBSITE

READ	+	LISTEN	+	WATCH
PRAYERS & POSTS TO MOVE YOU FORWARD		PODCAST + OTHER TRANSFORMATION RESOURCES		VIDEOS FOR EACH LESSON ONGOING TRAINING

1. Identity

Main idea: My uniqueness is a gift from God Himself. I matter because of who I am, more so than anything I do. The impact I make on the world is an overflow of who I am.

1. Begin by looking at life from a different perspective.

   A. Jesus preached that people should repent.

   - Matthew says the first thing Jesus preached— after the temptation— was this: "From that time Jesus began to preach and to say, 'Repent, for the Kingdom of Heaven is at hand'" (Matthew 4:17 NKJV).

     - Notice that Jesus did not call people to "repent or go to hell," to repent lest something horrible happen to them. He called them to repent… because the Kingdom was present.

     - The Greek word Jesus used was *metanoia*, a term which means "to change your mind," and "to see things differently."[1]

   ---

   [1] https://wordsmith.org/words/metanoia.html, accessed 2022-06-01

- Jesus invited people to see something they hadn't seen, so they might live a reality they had not yet lived— but was available to them.

- In other words, His message of "repent" was somewhat different than how we generally interpret it. **He encouraged people to "change their point-of-view" and see that the Kingdom was present**— that a better way of living is here!

REPENT

metanoia / Greek

PRONUNCIATION: (met-uh-NOI-uh)

MEANING: noun: A profound transformation in one's outlook.

ETYMOLOGY: From Greek *metanoia* (a change of mind), from *metanoein* (to change one's mind).

USAGE: "You'll need to rethink everything."

- When He sent the disciples to preach, Jesus instructed them (Matthew 10:7-8 NKJV, emphasis added).

  *And as you go, preach, saying, "**The kingdom of heaven is at hand."** Heal the sick, cleanse the lepers, raise the dead, cast out demons. Freely you have received, freely give.*

- Jesus said things like:

  - **The Kingdom is already here** (see Luke 17:21 NLT):

    *You won't be able to say, "Here it is!" or "It's over there!" For **the Kingdom of God is already among you.***

- **The message of the Kingdom is good news** (Mark 1:15 NIV):

  *"The time has come," He said. "**The kingdom of God has come near**. Repent and believe the good news!"*[2]

B. When you were "born again," here's what happened: you were awakened to see the Good News of the Gospel, including a revelation of who you really are!

- 1 Corinthians 15:34, "Awake to righteousness" (NKJV).

- Ephesians 5:14, "Awake, you who sleep" (NKJV).

C. Living with your "eyes wide open" always brings refreshing, because— again— the Gospel is Good News.

- At the first Pentecost sermon, Peter encouraged the crowd clearly that when we repent, we open the door for the Holy Spirit to come and bring times of refreshing (Acts 2:38-40 NIV):

  Peter replied, "Repent and be baptized, every one of you, in the name of Jesus Christ for the forgiveness of your sins. And you will receive the gift of the Holy Spirit. The promise is for you and your children and for all who are far off—for all whom the Lord our God will call."

- In Acts 3:19 we see the same pattern (NIV):

  Repent, then, and turn to God, so that your sins may be wiped out, that times of refreshing may come from the Lord...

- Repentance is not just "being sorry." **Repentance is awakening to a way of life, a way of life in which refreshing and rejuvenation comes.**

- In fact, during His ministry **Jesus told us this refreshing was one of the reasons why He came** (John 10:10 NKJV):

---

[2] Notice here that the call to repentance is to see something that's good. *Repent* is not spoken from the standpoint of running from something horrible, but of embracing something that's great.

The thief does not come except to steal, and to kill, and to destroy. I have come that they may have life, and that they may have it more abundantly.

THREE STEPS SEEN IN ACTS

REPENT

AWAKEN TO A
GREATER REALITY

RECEIVE

THE PRESENCE & POWER
OF GOD COME NEAR

REFRESH

REAL WORLD
TRANSFORMATION

2. One of the greatest areas of repentance is awakening to who we are, to our true identity. That is, we need to see ourselves as God sees us.

Identity theft is a major problem in our culture. However, the problem we see in the natural mirrors an even greater issue in the supernatural. **People don't know who they are. The enemy comes and steals their true identity. Then, he imposes a false one.**

Don't be a victim of "spiritual identity theft." Remember who you are.

We look at Creation and marvel. And rightly so. The Bible tells us that the Heavens declare the glory of God (Psalm 19:1). All of Creation reveals Him, in fact (Romans 8:18-25).

A. You are a work of art— and have been since before time began.

- Paul says that "[You] are His workmanship... created for good works He planned before hand [before time began] that you would walk in" (Ephesians 2:10 AMP).

- Notably, this is in the same passage as Ephesians 2:8 ("By grace you are saved..."). **The same grace that transforms you from sin to light is the exact same grace that has a destiny for you.** Your salvation and the purposes you walk in are not separate concepts.

- The word *workmanship* here is the Greek word *poema*, a word used of art, craftsmanship, and poetry. It's the imagery of a master-designer creating something extraordinary.

- We see this same concept throughout the Bible— that God creates people with a design and a destiny.

  - God informed Jeremiah (Jeremiah 1:5 NIV):

    Before I formed you in the womb I knew you, before you were born I set you apart; I appointed you as a prophet to the nations.

- Psalm 139:13-16 says much the same thing (MSG):

    Oh yes, you shaped me first inside, then out;

    you formed me in my mother's womb.

    I thank you, High God—you're breathtaking!

    Body and soul, I am marvelously made!

    I worship in adoration—what a creation!

    You know me inside and out,

    you know every bone in my body;

    You know exactly how I was made, bit by bit,

    how I was sculpted from nothing into something.

    Like an open book, you watched me grow from conception to birth;

    all the stages of my life were spread out before you,

    The days of my life all prepared

    before I'd even lived one day.

B. You have a unique design, a special bent given to you by God. This design affects every area of life.

- Proverbs 22:6 tells us, "Train up a child in the way they should go, and when they're older they won't depart from it."

    - Pastors and spiritual leaders teach that this verse promises a spiritual boomerang of sorts— "Raise kids with a moral compass, in the Christian faith, and— even if they sway away in their teen or young adult years— they'll eventually return to the faith."

    - Thankfully this dynamic occurs. If— and when— we veer off-course, God calls us back to Himself. However, this verse highlights another truth entirely.

- The word-imagery in the original Hebrew language of the Old Testament relates to buildings— of blueprints and architectural designs. Solomon (the author of the verse) contends that **in the same way engineers and craftsmen create cities and skylines with intentionality and purpose, so also God takes the same care in His craft of creating people.**

  - In effect, this Proverb tells us, "Your child has a specific design, a purpose all their own. Identify that when they're young. When they're older, they'll walk in that purpose. And they'll be all the better for it."

  - In other words, "Train up a child in their unique design, according to their blueprint…"

- This manual has been created with adults in mind. Remember, all adults were once children— and were given (by God) a unique bent, a specific design. We each have a blueprint.

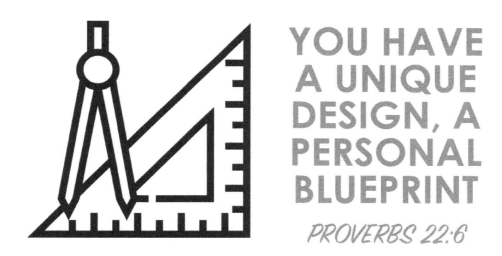

YOU HAVE A UNIQUE DESIGN, A PERSONAL BLUEPRINT

PROVERBS 22:6

- If you don't yet know your design, it's never too late to discover it, so you can walk in it. Remember, this is an important area of repentance— of seeing things from that different perspective.

C. Design determines destiny. When you understand how something is made, you understand what it was created to do.

- Walk through the tool corral in a hardware store and you'll quickly observe: there are hundreds of different kinds of tools. And, they each serve a different purpose. In fact, they were each invented for a specific purpose.

- In every instance the truth is the same: **Once you understand what the tool was created to do, you know what to do with it.**[3]

- To use the metaphor above, you're a tool. I'm a tool. And when we understand how and why the tool was designed, we know what to do with it.

3. Seven different designs highlight the Father's intentions for each of us. They describe how we were each made (and, thus, link to our purpose).

A. The Father, the Son, and the Spirit each have gifts.

- **Many believers are familiar with the gifts of the Holy Spirit.** The manifestations listed in 1 Corinthians 12:7-11 empower us to serve beyond our natural capacity, working in the power of the Holy Spirit (NJKV):

  > But **the manifestation of the Spirit is given to each one for the profit of all**: for to one is given the word of wisdom through the Spirit, to another the word of knowledge through the same Spirit, to another faith by the same Spirit, to another gifts of healings by the same Spirit, to another the working of miracles, to another prophecy, to another discerning of spirits, to another different kinds of tongues, to another the interpretation of tongues. **But one and the same Spirit works all these things**, distributing to each one individually as He wills.

---

[3] Hardwood floor nailers are terrible for framing houses. Screwdrivers are a miserable way to install a fence. But when each of these tools are used for their designed purpose, they make work faster, easier, and more of a delight than a drudge.

- **The Son also has gifts.** The five-fold ministry offices listed in Ephesians 4:11-13 are people whom Jesus gives to the church in order to help the people in the church find and fulfill their purpose. These "embodied" gifts (read: these people) help us reach maturity (NKJV):

  *And He Himself gave some to be apostles, some prophets, some evangelists, and some pastors and teachers, **for the equipping of the saints for the work of ministry**, for the edifying of the body of Christ, till we all come to the unity of the faith and of the knowledge of the Son of God, to a perfect man, **to the measure of the stature of the fullness of Christ.***

- **The Father also has gifts.** Romans 12:6-8 highlights seven motivational tendencies which describe our innate tendencies to interact with people and circumstances in unique ways (NKJV):

  Having then gifts differing according to the grace that is given to us, let us use them: if prophecy, let us prophesy in proportion to our faith; or ministry, let us use it in our ministering; he who teaches, in teaching; he who exhorts, in exhortation; he who gives, with liberality; he who leads, with diligence; he who shows mercy, with cheerfulness.

GIFTS OF THE FATHER
ROMANS 12:6-8

Prophecy
Service
Teaching
Exhortation
Giving
Leading
Mercy

GIFTS OF THE SON
EPHESIANS 4:11-13

Apostles
Prophets
Evangelists
Pastors
Teachers

GIFTS OF THE SPIRIT
I CORINTHIANS 12:7-11

Word of Wisdom
Word of Knowledge
Faith
Healing
Miracles
Prophecy
Discerning Spirits
Tongues
Interpretation of Tongues

- The gifts arrive at different times in our lives— and for different reasons.

  - You receive the gifts of the Spirit when you become a Christian— when the Holy Spirit moves into your life.

  - You receive the gifts of the Son when you connect with a faith community.

  - You receive the gifts of the Father simply for being born. They are part of that unique Proverbs 22:6 bent.

GIFTS OF THE SPIRIT
MANIFESTATIONS, TO SERVE
BEYOND OUR NATURAL CAPACITY
1 CORINTHIANS 12:7-11

GIFTS OF THE SON
TO BRING US TO MATURITY,
HELP US FIND OUR PURPOSE
EPHESIANS 4:11-12

GIFTS OF THE FATHER
HIGHLIGHT OUR MOTIVATION
(OR, INHERENT DRIVE)
ROMANS 12:6-8

B. You naturally lean towards one or two of the seven gifts of the Father.

- Above, Paul lists the 7 in Romans 12:6-8:

  1. Prophecy

2. Service

3. Teaching

4. Exhorting

5. Giving

6. Leading (or Ruling)

7. Mercy

- **When you were created, these came with the package.** In fact, after studying this lesson, you're going to understand a lot about you— and about the people closest to you!

C. The Creation story illustrates how these gifts work.

Over the next few pages, let's evaluate each of the seven creative gifts from the Creation story. We'll cover them in the order they appear.[4] We'll explain them and provide you with a Biblical example of each one.

1. **Prophecy— God spoke creation into existence, using His words to bring about created order (Genesis 1:3-5). In the same way, some people have unique design whereby they can create order and destiny with their words!**

    - We see this on Day 1— and on every day thereafter. The refrain throughout Genesis 1 is "Let there be…" and then there is!

    - Some people have a unique ability to speak into chaos and call forth life and design— even destiny. They can call things that are "not" and things that are not as they should be— and bring the gold forth!

---

[4] By the way, you'll see these seven gifts outlined throughout the entire Bible in various ways. In fact, we find 100+ lists of sevens in the Bible, each of them outlined in the same order as the Romans 12 gifts. (Go to https://sevensinthebible.com/list-of-sevens-in-the-bible/, accessed 06-17-2022).

In this book we'll study:
- Seven pillars of wisdom. One scholar identifies these as counsel, knowledge, understanding, might or strength, power or authority, riches and honor. See http://www.biblescholars.org/2013/05/proverbs-91.html
- Seven churches in Revelation
- Seven sayings of Jesus from the Cross

You may have attributes of all seven, but you'll predominantly lean towards one or two of these gifts.

- Proverbs tells us that life and death is in the power of the tongue (Proverbs 18:21). Anyone can condemn and diminish; some people have a profound ability to use the power of words to generate life!

- Biblical example— Peter. We see Peter address the crowd at Solomon's Porch (after healing the lame man while on the way to pray with John). When the crowd seeks an explanation for how the miracle happened, he declares to them their true identity as those who are destined to be blessed as well (see Acts 3:25).

2. **Service— On Day 2, God separated the firmament, dividing the water above the sky from the water below the sky (Genesis 1:6-8). Some people's design enables them to wash others— with words or deeds— in such a way that peace comes.**

   - Many people walk with a grace and humility that empowers them to cleanse and wash others, nourishing them in a profound manner. It never seems contrived; it always appears at the right time.

   - Notice how Paul says that husbands should love their wives in this way, washing them with the water of the word (see Ephesians 5:26).

   - Biblical example— Tabitha (also called Dorcas) is the first person we see resurrected after Jesus' ascension (see Acts 9:36f.). The Scripture tells us that after her death, the Church was deeply saddened. We read that she spent most of her days making tunics and garments for the widows in their community (see Acts 9:39).

   - Note: serving doesn't have to be "making something" for someone. For instance, we read about Judas, the man who invited Saul into his home after his Damascus road experience. Though he receives only one line of text in the Scripture, he obviously played a pivotal role (see Acts 9:11).

3. **Teaching— On Day 3, God separated the water that covered the face of the earth, creating land masses (1:9-10). Then, He spoke forth trees and other seed-bearing plants (1:11-13). In the same way that trees bear**

seeds which continue bearing fruit, some people have a design that enables them to speak nuggets of truth that empowers others to either bear fruit or find spiritual refuge.

- Each tree carries unlimited potential for growth. For instance, when an apple tree blossoms its apples, each apple contains numerous seeds- meaning each individual fruit from a tree has unlimited potential itself!

- Some people teach and expound upon truths in a unique way, multiplying revelation and insight, making it simple and accessible to others. Rather than living "in the clouds," as some intellects do, these people have the ability to continually produce "low-hanging fruit" that others can easily grasp. The gift of teaching doesn't make things more complex; it makes truths more accessible.

- Biblical example— the Apostle John. The Bible tells us that Jesus did so many things during His ministry that the world could not contain the books that would be written (John 21:25). Obviously, this is an exaggeration, but it makes the point. Jesus did a lot! However, John boils down the essence of what Jesus did into a Gospel that, really, you can read in about 45 minutes. It contains some of the most quoted passages in the entire Bible. As well, the short letters he penned to his churches distill the essence of Christianity to two actions steps, walking in love and light.

4. **Exhorting— On Day 4, God called forth the sun, the moon, and the stars (1:14-19). We read that everything in the Heavens was created by Him and continually declares His glory (Psalm 19:1). Some people have an incredible ability to call forth the glory of God in people, so that they shine like stars in the universe (see Philippians 2:15).**

- People with this design literally encourage others in such a way that they call forth the glory that resides in each of us.

- In Christian circles, we often focus on the "negative" side of accountability (i.e., making sure people don't do the things they aren't supposed to do- things they should stay away from). True encouragers walk with a worldview that causes them to call forth the destiny of people by naturally encouraging them to be the person they're designed to be (the positive side of accountability). They bring hope alive!

- Biblical example— Barnabas. When the Early Church was a young movement and had few resources, Barnabas sold a field and gave the apostles the money (see Acts 4:36f.). Then, he was also able to see in Paul what others couldn't see (Acts 9:26-30). Later, when John Mark bailed out on a mission trip, Paul refused to take the young man on the next one— but Barnabas stood by him and took the young leader along with him, splitting with Paul (Acts 15:39-41). Apparently, Mark grew into his role. Paul called for him as he was aging (see 2 Timothy 4:11), and Mark went on to pen the first Gospel that was published.[5]

5. **Giving— On Day 5, God spoke forth the fish and the birds— then every other living animal (1:20-25). In the animals, we see relationships begin to take place— something that, until this point, is unique in the world. Some people have a true gift of giving— a way of extending of themselves in a way that overflows with life and grace.**

   - Animals began caring for each other in a special way, connecting in groups in a different way than how plants did. Whereas plants do have symbiotic relationships with one another, animals create habitats, gather food for their young, and give of themselves in a special way.[6]

   - Some people have a true gift of giving— a way of extending of themselves in a way that overflows with life and grace. In the same way that parents don't consider what they are "giving" when they tend to their young, these people never see it as a loss when they extend

[5] Most historians believe Mark was written before Matthew. And, they believe Matthew and Luke actually used Mark's outline as the basis for their own narratives.

[6] Even in an urban area— in a concrete jungle— a bird will create a safe habitat for their young, using trash and debris to create a palace where others can flourish!

themselves to others- particularly when leveraging resources to empower someone else.[7]

- Biblical example— King David earnestly wanted to build a temple for God. However, the Lord promised him that it wouldn't happen in his time- that his kingdom would be firmly established, but that a son of his would build the Temple since he wasn't so occupied with war as David had been. His response? David made all of the plans and raised all of the provisions for the temple so that the next generation could easily build something he would never see (see 1 Chronicles 28-29).

6. **Ruling— On Day 6, God created man and woman in His image (1:26-30). He gave them a unique position to steward all of creation— to, in effect, make it better by their presence. Of course, there are people with a unique design whereby they do this at an extremely high level!**

   - Man & woman were given dominion and authority over all of creation. Adam was given authority to name the animals. Eve was known as the "mother of all the living," even before she birthed a child (Genesis 3:20).

   - All humans have dominion— it's who we are. However, some people have a special ability to lead and to exercise authority in such a way that things are better because they are there. Whereas all people are destined to "reign in life" (Romans 5:17), these individuals often create order that empowers them to do it and then point the way.

   - Biblical example— Peter. Peter did what a lot of leaders do— he acted impulsively— jumping out of the boat to walk on water (Matthew 14:22-23), rebuking Jesus (Matthew 16:22), even telling Jesus he would die with Him (Matthew 26:35). This same boldness was present in the Upper Room when a disciple was chosen to replace Matthias (Acts 1:15), as well as when he stood and made sense of the outpouring of the Holy Spirit at Pentecost (Acts 2:14).

---

[7] Note: you don't have to be wealthy to have this gift of giving! Some people are wired to be generous!

7. **Mercy— We read that on Day 7 God rested from His labor (1:31). He saw that all of His work was good, and then He ceased working- for the day. This was a unique moment, because later Jesus tell us that the Father continues working even now (John 5:17).**

   - By their very presence, some individuals bring others into a place of *rest*. They have a gift of saying the right thing, creating the right environment, or simply being present… and it puts others at peace.

   - Often, these people can create a "holy moment" at any time and place- just by the mantle they carry. As a result, people feel comforted, at peace, and their strength is renewed….

   - Biblical example— Though he uses words to convey this, James (Jesus' brother) seems to be a man of mercy. If you read his epistle, you may get the idea that he's all "black and white." However, the way James responds at the Jerusalem Council is profound. When the question was posed as to whether or not circumcision and other elements of the Law would be required for Gentile converts, James is the one who created peace by laying few requirements on them (see Acts 15:13-21).

DAYS OF CREATION = THE FATHER'S GIFTS

1- PROPHECY   speak what should be

2 - SERVICE   bring order by helping

3 - TEACHING   find seeds that grow into life

4- EXHORTING   awaken hope & courage

5 - GIVING   overflow tangible grace to others

6 - RULING   show the way & empower improvement

7- MERCY   create sacred space for rest

4. These gifts explain why you are the way you are and why you do things the way you do. So, embrace your design, *and* celebrate the differences of others.

Don't make someone feel bad because they're different than you. Don't feel less valuable because of the design you have. The truth is that we all need each other. Every person— and every design— is important.

A. You can probably identify your creative design by evaluating how you've naturally responded in past situations— or how you would respond to a hypothetical one.

- Notice how you might respond to an everyday situation— let's say you're at a birthday party and, at the pivotal moment, *someone drops the cake!*

  - **Prophet—** will likely speak out and say something intended to be encouraging that might come across as judgey if they're not careful: "If you weren't in such a hurry, this wouldn't have happened."

  - **Servant—** will probably not say anything at all. They'll just begin cleaning up the mess.

  - **Teacher—** might evaluate for a moment and then speak analytically: "If you'll just rearrange the furniture…" They may even provide suggestions as to how to do it.

  - **Exhorter—** just wants the party to continue. Cake or no cake, everyone's here— let's keep celebrating!

  - **Giver—** might actually run to the store to buy another cake- without being asked.

  - **Ruler—** begins telling everyone what to do.

  - **Mercy—** consoles the person who dropped the cake and/or the person being celebrated. (They may say something like, "Ahh… I've dropped cakes before…").

- With this mental framework, **you can probably recall other instances in your life where you've seen different designs at work.** Rather than creating a source of tension and conflict, we can embrace our differences!

IN EVERYDAY LIFE, EVERY GIFT MATTERS

1- PROPHET Speaks immediately

2 - SERVANT Doesn't speak- starts cleaning

3 - TEACHER Analyzes how to prevent this again

4- EXHORTER Encourages the party to continue

5 - GIVER Is on the way to get another cake

6 - RULE Tells everyone what to do

7- MERCY Consoles the person

- Furthermore, **the gift needed the most often changes based on the situation.** Consider…

    - Which design is most needed at the scene of a fatal accident?

    - Which design best leads— or coaches— a Little League team?

    - Which design plans the best party?

    - Which best facilitates a group project?

B. In everyday life, every design is needed. And, in ministry, each design is valuable as well.

- We don't want to judge others for how they're created— we obviously need every design.

- And, we don't want to mold our spouses or kids into someone they're not. We want to celebrate who God made them— they fulfill a purpose we can't.

- We want to remember **we're better together— particularly when we all function from our different strengths.**

- We want to remember what motivates others. Many conflicts are caused just by not understanding how others are wired.

C. Remember, though, your value is based in whose you are— not in your design or your successful execution of your gift (in fact, each design exhibits its own "legitimacy lie," which tells us we're valuable once we achieve something specific).

- Your identity has already been settled by what Jesus achieved for you!

- The value something has is revealed by how much someone is willing to pay for that item. For example:

  - Willie Nelson's hair braids were sold for $37,000.[8]

  - William Shatner auctioned off *part* of his kidney stone to raise money for Habitat for Humanity in 2006. He raised $25,000.

  - A lock of Elvis Presley's hair sold for $115,000 in 2002!

  - After blowing her nose on The Tonight Show, Scarlett Johansen sold the tissue for $5,000.[9]

  - One of Napoleon's signature two-pointed hats sold for $2.2 million![10]

- Whether or not we look at something and believe it has value or not, the value is based on what someone will pay for it.

- Notice what the Bible says about your value (1 Peter 1:18-19 NASB):

---

[8] http://www.cnn.com/2014/10/09/showbiz/gallery/celebrity-auctions/

[9] https://www.scoopwhoop.com/inothernews/weird-celebrity-auction/#.db2qntfo1

[10] http://www.dailysabah.com/life/2015/02/04/auctioned-weird-belongings-of-famous-people

You were not redeemed with perishable things like silver or gold from your futile way of life inherited from your forefathers, but with precious blood, as of a lamb unblemished and spotless, the blood of Christ.

5. Develop your design by becoming aware of the potential hindrances to your destiny, the complete redemption you have through Christ, and the ultimate destiny for you.

    A. Each design has a potential pitfall, as well as a bountiful blessing. We need to be aware of both.

- **The "Legitimacy Lie" denotes the primary means we wrongly think we can use to attain value or position based on what we do— apart from who we are and whose we are.** Each redemptive gift, falls prey to a different temptation in this area. We read, "When we do not find our legitimacy in God, we begin to seek it from other people or through our accomplishments."[11]

- **The "Potential Pitfall," as we'll call it (sometimes referred to as a "root iniquity") is the sin common to most people with this gift-type.** If we know this tactic, then see it emerging in our lives, we can quickly break this tendency.

    B. These gift-types are often known as "Redemptive gifts" because we see their initial potential in the Creation story (then, we know the Fall occurred, followed by their complete redemption at the Cross).

- **Jesus' 7 sayings at the Cross correspond to each of the 7 gift types.** Like the corresponding days of Creation, we find these in the same order as the Romans 12:6-8 passage.

---

[11] See Wale's *Designed for Fulfillment*, page 45.

- **These 7 gifts are often called "Redemptive Gifts," because Jesus redeemed them from their pitfall and into their potential at the Cross.** His words from the Cross show the redemption— and the path forward— for each gift.

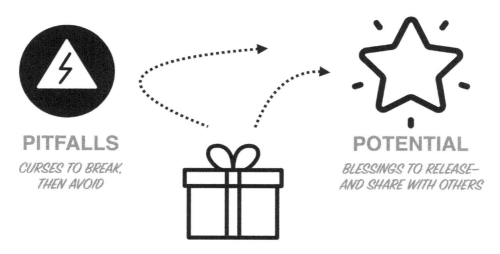

EVERY GIFT CARRIES MULTIPLE POSSIBILITIES...

PITFALLS
CURSES TO BREAK,
THEN AVOID

POTENTIAL
BLESSINGS TO RELEASE-
AND SHARE WITH OTHERS

C. **The Bible outlines the power of each of these seven in numerous ways.**

- **Whereas we want to "break off" the curses, we want position ourselves receive the blessings.** Each of these correspond to an Old Testament leader who opposed the enemy's of God's people.[12]

- **The 7 churches in Revelation each correspond to a gift, as well, showing us the supernatural destiny of each of the gifts.** This shows "another revelation of what God puts in our spiritual DNA" and highlights our destiny when we walk in spiritual wholeness.[13]

---

[12] *Designed for Fulfillment*, page 44.

[13] *Designed for Fulfillment*, page 40.

Transform: Identity

Following each chapter of this manual, you'll find a place to apply what you've just learned. As the title of this book suggests, **we're not only looking to learn information, we're seeking life transformation.**

1. Follow the link below and take the Redemptive Gifts Assessment. Though a "test" or assessment instrument isn't the ultimate determination of your gift-mix, it can provide you with a great place to begin exploration.

    (Final confirmation should come from what you hear the Holy Spirit say, as well as what you find in the Scripture, and what other trusted bothers and sisters in Christ affirm.)

2. After taking the assessment, follow the links related to your suggested gift-mix and make a few notes as to what you see, sense, or feel about your identity. What parts of the assessment seem accurate? What seems inaccurate? Write your thoughts below.

3. Follow the links to learn more about your gift. Then pray (out loud) the curses off and the blessings on your life. Make notes below where you have seen the curses or blessings operating in your life.

_____

_____

_____

_____

_____

_____

_____

_____

_____

_____

_____

_____

4. Learn more about each of the gifts from the links below and the pages that follow.

Note: you'll want to learn more about each of the gifts, as your spouse, your friends, and your family members will likely have a radically different mix than you. And, this is by God's design!

Contents of Redemptive Gifts

Note: in this portion of the book we'll leave heavily on Charles R. Wale's book, *Designed for Fulfillment: A Study of the Redemptive Gifts*. Look at the footnotes for specific page numbers if you wish to take a deeper dive into his materials.

5. Review the teaching on Identity here. Use the space below to make any notes you wish to remember or study further. The talk is available at the link below:

_____

_____

_____

_____

_____

_____

_____

_____

_____

Overview

Creation
Each design mirrors one of the days of Creation. Remarkably, the redemptive gifts, as we refer to them, follow the same order in Romans 12:6-8 as they appear in the Creation story.

The Principle
Seven principles of wisdom appear in Proverbs 9:1, each of the principles matching one of the redemptive gifts. Again, these appear in the same order. Solomon, the attributed author of Proverbs, tells us, "Wisdom has herein her house. She has hewn out its seven pillars…"[14]

The Legitimacy Lie
The "Legitimacy Lie" denotes the primary means we wrongly think we can use to attain value or position based on what we do. Each redemptive gift falls prey to a different temptation in this area. "When we do not find our legitimacy in God, we begin to seek it from other people in in accomplishments."[15]

The Enemy's Tactic
Sometimes referred to as "the curse," the Israelites faced 7 enemies as they walked into their inheritance, the Promised Land. Each enemy denotes one of the 7 arch-nemeses of the gifts. These curses (read: these enemies) can keep us from fulfilling our true destiny.[16]

Potential Pitfall
The "root iniquity" is the sin common to most people with this gift-type. If we know this tactic then see it emerging in our lives, we can quickly break this tendency.

---

[14] Each of us are created in God's image. As such, we each reflect a facet of this wisdom— of His image. (Jesus embodied each of the gifts of the Son we see in Ephesians 4:11-13, and the Holy Spirit manifests each of the spiritual gifts we find in 1 Corinthians 12:7-11).

[15] See Wale's *Designed for Fulfillment*, page 45.

[16] *Designed for Fulfillment*, page 43. A curse can come from words, from a broken covenant, or from disobedience.

The Cross

Jesus' 7 sayings at the Cross correspond to each of the 7 gift types. Like the corresponding days of Creation, we find these in the same order as the Romans 12:6-8 passage. These 7 gifts are often called "Redemptive Gifts," because Jesus redeemed them from their pitfall and into their potential at the Cross. His words from the Cross show the redemption— and the path forward— for each.

The Blessings

Whereas we want to "break off" the curses, we want to position ourselves to receive the blessings. Each of these correspond to an Old Testament leader who opposed the enemy's of God's people.[17]

The Tabernacle

The 7 articles of furniture in the Tabernacle— the place where God's manifest presence fell— also offer insight into each of the gifts. Again, they appear in the same order.

The Birthright / Destiny

The 7 churches in Revelation each correspond to a gift, showing us the supernatural destiny of each of the gifts. This shows "another revelation of what God puts in our spiritual DNA" and highlights our destiny when we walk in spiritual wholeness.[18]

When we walk in our true destiny, we get a feeling that "This is who I am. This is who God made me. This is what God made me for. I was born for this, and I am accomplishing what God called me to do."[19]

Person to Study

For each gift we'll also reference several characters in the Bible you can study for additional reference.

---

[17] *Designed for Fulfillment*, page 44.

[18] *Designed for Fulfillment*, page 40.

[19] *Designed for Fulfillment*, page 16.

1. Prophet

Creation
Day 1 = God spoke and creation came into order.

(The prophet has the highest authority over the poverty spirit, as the prophet carries a God-given capacity to speak order from chaos.[20])

The Principle
Design. The prophet can see order in God's Word and in His precepts. They desire to build their life—and the lives of others— around that. The prophet can also see God's unique calling— His stamp of identity— on another person, often calling it forth.[21]

The Legitimacy Lie
"I can solve my own problem and fix things better than God."[22]

The prophet feels important— and needed— when fixing broken things (especially people). When unhealthy, they can come across as judgey.

The Enemy's Tactic
Aramean curse (see Genesis 28-29).[23] Jacob worked 7 years for Laban in exchange for Rachel's hand in marriage. But, on the wedding night, Laban swapped brides— and Jacob didn't know until he consummated the marriage. Laban, an Aramean, didn't trust God to provide a suitable husband for Leah— the older, less attractive daughter. So, he solved the problem in his own strength.

Potential Pitfall
Can be ruled by anger when others don't fall in line— and can become hyper-critical.

---

[20] *Designed for Fulfillment*, page 48.

[21] *Designed for Fulfillment*, page 48

[22] *Designed for Fulfillment*, page 50.

[23] *Designed for Fulfillment*, page 50

The Cross

Luke 23:34, "Father forgive them, for they know not what they're doing."

A prophet's zeal might cause them to take up a cause against people. Rather, they should tenderly call God to move soon behalf of those people— not merely call people to step towards God.[24]

The Blessings

The prophet Hosea had an unfaithful wife. He had to hold her to God's standards, yet he did so graciously (see Hosea 2:2-13). In time, she turned her heart towards him, and she eventually referred to him with the endearing term "husband" rather than the cultural term "my master" (see Hosea 2:14-16).[25]

The Tabernacle

The brazen altar is the first piece a worshipper would see in the Tabernacle (see Exodus 27:1-8, 38:1-17). This is where God cleared sin, so they could go further in the relationship. This was the starting point to walking in true spiritual depth— not the finish line.[26] In the same way, the prophet brings confession of sin— not condemnation. That is, a prophet points to the sacrifice— not the person's shortcomings.

The Birthright / Destiny

A prophet's destiny, their true spiritual DNA, is to help others see their true identity— to see themselves as God sees them. They call forth the Kingdom greatness inside of others, such that it shines forth. The church at Ephesus is the example from the Book of Revelation (see Revelation 2:-17). They couldn't tolerate wickedness, they persevered, and they overcome. However, they were in danger of losing their first love— of becoming more enamored at pointing out shortcomings than staying enraptured by the Savior.

Person to Study

Caleb, Elijah, Ezekiel, Miriam, Peter

---

24 *Designed for Fulfillment*, page 54.

25 *Designed for Fulfillment*, page 52.

26 *Designed for Fulfillment*, page 53.

2. Servant

Creation
Day 2 = God separated the waters, creating a new atmosphere where everything else to come could reach its full potential.

The Principle
Authority. The servant enjoys helping others reach their full potential by coming beneath them. As such, God entrusts them with great influence because they don't crave the attention and power for their own use.[27]

The Legitimacy Lie
"I am legitimate when I build a platform of success under others."[28]

A servant can develop a "savior mentality" of being valuable only when needed by someone else— if they don't find their true identity in God.

The Enemy's Tactic
Moabite curse (see Judges 3:12-30). The Moabites controlled the trade route at Jericho, prohibiting the Israelites from moving freely for commerce. The Moabite curse, broken when Ehud slaughtered the Moabite king (3:29) causes people in authority to suppress and limit the freedom of those under them.[29]

Potential Pitfall
Embracing peace at any cost, as well as not seeing proper boundaries with other people.[30]

---

[27] *Designed for Fulfillment*, page 58.

[28] *Designed for Fulfillment*, page 60.

[29] *Designed for Fulfillment*, page 60.

[30] *Designed for Fulfillment*, pages 58 and 61.

The Cross

Luke 23:43, "Today, you will be with Me in paradise."

The thief had nothing to offer Jesus— yet Jesus saw him as God the Father does. He facilitated the repentant man's transition forward into the Kingdom of God.[31] Servants do this. They agree with God, and they confirm what they see with the washing of the water of the Word (see also Ephesians 5:26).

The Blessings

The blessing of Esther. Though she was orphaned when she was young— and then raised by her uncle— she served behind the scenes, unseen by most, and saved an entire people group. She acted shrewdly— even if initially hesitant.[32]

The Tabernacle

The second item a worshipper in the Tabernacle met after the brazen altar the bronze laver. Water was available to the priests, as well as to cleanse the sacrifice (see Exodus 29:4, 30:17-21, 38:8).[33]

Notice the progress. Worshippers moved from the sacrifice towards the throne room (the mercy seat). The washing along the way was an essential step.

The Birthright / Destiny

The Church at Smyrna (see Revelation 2:8-11). God saw their works, their struggles, and even their poverty that no one else saw. They persisted faithfully.

A servant works behind the scenes— and may go unnoticed (while the people they serve go very noticed). God promises that He always sees, and He gives these servants the crown of life.

Person to Study

Ananias (who helped Paul after the Damascus Road conversion), Barnabas, Esther, Timothy

---

[31] *Designed for Fulfillment,* page 64.

[32] *Designed for Fulfillment,* page 63.

[33] *Designed for Fulfillment,* page 64.

3. Teacher

Creation
Day 3 = seed-bearing plants were created, each seed having unlimited potential to continue multiplying indefinitely. The teacher has the highest authority over the predator spirit. Jesus told a parable of a sower and his seeds, and the devil was represented by the birds that came and devoured seed (see Mark 4:4, 15).

The Principle
Responsibility. Teachers find it easy to overlook responsibility in some areas, as well as overlooking their personal responsibility to take action. They can become information heavy instead of implementation-leaning.

The Legitimacy Lie
"I know the truth, and it gives me power. I am legitimate when I have complete and accurate information. I am legitimate— and I am right with God— when I know more."[34] This lie can become a stronghold that morphs into a "religious spirit." Recall, in the story of the Good Samaritan, the people who bypassed the wounded traveler in need… were teachers. They were on their way to exercise their religious duties and overlooked the responsibility (Luke 10:25-37).

The Enemy's Tactic
Philistine curse (see 1 Samuel 13:17-22). During this time period, the Israelites weren't allowed to have weapons— just gardening tools. Often, a teacher lacks one key resource— they need to get the job done. But, if they'll pursue intimacy rather than just information, God will unlock supernatural strategy to them.[35]

Potential Pitfall
Selective responsibility.[36] They might take responsibility in some areas, but avoid others— feeling as if they've done their part. They can become entitled, as well.

---

[34] *Designed for Fulfillment,* page 72.

[35] *Designed for Fulfillment,* page 72. See Genesis 26:12f., when Isaac sowed and reaped 100-fold during a famine.

[36] *Designed for Fulfillment,* page 71.

The Cross

John 19:26-27, "Behold your mother…"

At the Cross, Jesus gave John— a teacher— a specific responsibility of not only transmitting supernatural information to others but also living out the ramifications of God's principles for himself. [37]

The Blessings

Daniel. He refused to step into a human based power-play with others. He continued seeking the Lord intimately amidst the trial. When a teacher seeks the Lord not only for information but also for intimacy, the supernatural strategies flow.[38]

The Tabernacle

The showbread was the third item in the Tabernacle progression (see Exodus 35:23-30, 37:10-16). Through it, God revealed who He is (Jesus is the bread of life and the Word to be consumed), as well as who His people were (12 loaves represented the 12 tribes).

Frankincense was also available on the same table, which represented worship. This is always our right response— intimate worship— to the revelation we see of God. Information and intimacy work together.[39]

The Birthright / Destiny

Pergammum is the church in Revelation that denotes this gift (Revelation 2:12-17). This church was tested and didn't renounce their faith. They were told to pursue the deepest truths, which can only be known through intimacy. If they lacked anything it could be found in the secret place with the Lord— and be learned intimately not informationally. They were promised hidden manna (i.e., special supernatural food) for their pursuit.

Person to Study

John, Luke

---

[37] *Designed for Fulfillment*, page 77.

[38] *Designed for Fulfillment*, page 74.

[39] *Designed for Fulfillment*, page 76.

4. Exhorter

Creation
Day 4 = the stars were made to proclaim the glory of God. Exhorters have this as their nature— to call out the glory in others. They can draw large crowds and be seen by many (like the stars), spreading God's Word and His glory broadly.

The Principle
Sowing and reaping. Exhorters can quickly bounce from one idea to the next, never staying on one thing long enough to truly reap the benefits and see a result. They need to learn to invest now for the future and to persist through the entire process.[40]

The Legitimacy Lie
"I am legitimate when people want and need to be around me."[41]

The true exhorter isn't a person looking for a party; they are a party waiting to happen. As such, they find rejection difficult to swallow.

The Enemy's Tactic
Canaanite curse (Genesis 9:18-27).[42] Canaan saw his father, Noah, naked. Rather than covering him, he showed his brothers— seeking to please his brothers, and getting them to lower their standards. As a result, he was punished to stay in the hill country ratter than the fertile land— where sowing was more difficult. When the Israelites later went into the Promised Land, they found it hard to drive out the Canaanites and settle, because the Canaanites had iron chariots.

Potential Pitfall
Can be a people pleaser, as well as give up when things become a struggle. They don't like the time between the sowing and the reaping— and readily bounce prematurely.

---

[40] *Designed for Fulfillment*, page 84.

[41] *Designed for Fulfillment*, page 85.

[42] *Designed for Fulfillment*, page 86.

The Cross

Matthew 27:46, "My God, My God, why have You forsaken Me..."

On the Cross, Jesus felt the separation between Himself and the Father. Though we will never be separated from God, exhorters must learn to not base their interpretation of what God is doing on external circumstances alone. There's always a time of barrenness between sowing and reaping. They must learn to grow comfortable apart from circumstances.

The Blessings

Moses. Moses faced consistent demands from the people. He learned he could not stay around with them all— to please them. His father-in-law, Jethro, advised Him to work through others (see Exodus 18:1f.).[43] In turn, Moses had enough time to pursue intimacy with God, lead the people well, write 5 books of the Old Testament, and outline the detailed laws and directives for worship. In all, he spent 80 years in the wilderness to do so.

The Tabernacle

The fourth item in the Tabernacle was the golden lamp stand with the oils (Exodus 25:31-40, 37:17-24). The light illuminated the path forward and represented the revelation of God's nature. The oils were painstakingly prepared, just like the principle of sowing and reaping— and were necessary for the process to work.[44]

The Birthright / Destiny

Thyatira (see Revelation 3:19-29) was a church known well by Jesus for their reputation of good works. They revealed God to others in doing so. They were doing more than many others— they were busy. He encouraged them that it's not just about "doing more," but it's about finishing and being faithful all the way to the end. Those who endured would be given the Morning Star.[45]

Person to Study

Moses, Paul, John Mark

---

[43] esigned for Fulfillment, page 88.

[44] Designed for Fulfillment, page 89.

[45] Designed for Fulfillment, page 91.

5. Giver

Creation
Day 5 = many of the animals who nurture and care for each other in a far more symbiotic way than plants, giving of themselves appear.

The Principle
Stewardship, that is, faithfully managing something that is not yours on behalf of someone else.[46] This can produce the stronghold of fear (there's not enough). Ownership also creates strongholds— like arrogance (look what I have, that I acquired with my ability) and control (I'll manipulate others with my resources, based on what I share or don't share).

The Legitimacy Lie
"I can provide the resources for others to possess their birthright— that is, to walk in their destiny. I am legitimate when I am needed... for the resources."[47]

The fruit of this lie can become, rather quickly, codependency. Stewardship might not relate only to money. Sometimes, it includes the creative use of all resources, multiplying them to achieve far more than dreamed possible, such as the boy with 5 loaves and 2 fish (John 6:1-14).

The Enemy's Tactic
Midianite curse (Judges 6:1-6). They terrorized Israel, such that everyone fled their homes and lived in mountains and caves. Their resources— fields and livestock— were ravaged. Nothing was left behind for them.[48]

This might happen in cycles for someone under this curse.

Potential Pitfall
Control and manipulation, as well as codependency.

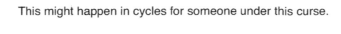

46 *Designed for Fulfillment,* page 96.

47 *Designed for Fulfillment,* page 98.

48 *Designed for Fulfillment,* page 98.

The Cross

John 19:28, "I thirst."

It's difficult for a giver to express need and then receive. But they must learn to do so.[49] As such, God wants to move them to the point where they realize there are greater treasures than early resources— which are merely tools to be used (see Luke 16:11).

The Blessings

Job was blessed with the ability to accumulate resources at supernatural speed, compressing the normal time and space required to do so. He lost everything at the beginning of his story (which is often the case for true givers— they overcome loss). In the end of his story, he owned twice as much as he did at the beginning.[50]

The Tabernacle

The Altar of Incense is the next article of furniture in the Tabernacle (see Exodus 30:1-10, 37:25-28). Here, we see intercession and worship fused together in total harmony. This moves us beyond busyness.[51] It moves us beyond the "stuff" of this world. We step into the true treasures of the Kingdom, with radical heart transformation (Matthew 6:21). When the heart is pure, everything on the planet can be managed for godly purposes (see Titus 1:15, 1 Timothy 4:4-5).

The Birthright / Destiny

The Church at Sardis (Revelation 3:1-6) had a reputation of been alive, but they were dead. On the outside they looked fine, but they were truly poor— inwardly.[52] Givers have a destiny to release blessings and multiply resources and to create systems that do so, but it must work from the "inside out." Givers must work to intentionally not create a reputation based on earthly abundance only, but on Heavenly substance.

Person to Study

Abraham, Jacob, Job, Matthew

---

[49] *Designed for Fulfillment,* page 102.

[50] *Designed for Fulfillment,* page 100.

[51] *Designed for Fulfillment,* page 102.

[52] *Designed for Fulfillment,* page 102.

6. Ruler

Creation
Day 6 = God created man and woman, giving them stewardship over all Creation.

The Principle
Freedom. The ruler is a leader, an organizer, and an empire builder— and does so for God's purposes. They must leverage everything they do to facilitate freedom— not control. They must empower people, not restrain them.

The Legitimacy Lie
"I am legitimate when I am over people and have institutional authority."[53]

In other words, the ruler— when unhealthy— craves position.

The Enemy's Tactic
Jotham's curse (see Judges 9). Jotham rebelled against Abimelech, who had slaughtered 70 of his father's sons. Jotham escaped and then enticed Israel to overthrow the rebel who had overthrown his father. Abimelech was killed when a woman tossed a millstone over a tower, hitting him in the head.

The curse of Jotham often causes internal uprising and revolt, such that the ruler cannot move forward.[54]

Potential Pitfall
Leadership isn't based on title or position, but is rooted in God's supernatural providence and empowerment. Unhealthy rulers crave titles and posts rather than comfortably walking out their calling wherever God places them.

---

[53] *Designed for Fulfillment,* page 110.

[54] *Designed for Fulfillment,* page 110.

The Cross

John 19:30, "It is finished."

There is nothing more you must do to earn position— you have freedom and serve at a higher capacity knowing that God manages and holds the future. There's no burden on you to attain anything.[55]

The Blessings

Nehemiah organized a group of people to complete a human task (rebuilding the walls around Jerusalem) in record time. The timeline was seemingly impossible. He stepped forward even though he faced formidable enemies. In turn, God provided supernatural strategies and an abundance of resources to complete the project.[56]

The Tabernacle

The Ark appears next in the Tabernacle (see Exodus 25:10-16, 37:1-5). The Ark contained three items, particularly relevant to the ruler:

1. The 10 commandments, showing God's precepts and requirements

2. Manna, showing God's provision and His resources (even in the wilderness)

3. Aaron's rod that budded, showing God's people and relationships

The ruler leverages all three— precepts, provision, and people— to exercise their gift.[57]

The Birthright / Destiny

The Church at Philadelphia (Revelation 3:7-13) is said to have an open door that no one can close (even if no one else could see it). Others, false leaders, would see what God did through them, and take note. This is true of rulers and is their destiny, open doors.[58]

Person to Study

Boaz, Joseph, Nehemiah, Solomon

---

[55] *Designed for Fulfillment,* page 114.

[56] *Designed for Fulfillment,* page 112.

[57] *Designed for Fulfillment,* page 113.

[58] *Designed for Fulfillment,* page 115.

7. Mercy

Creation
Day 7 = God ordained a day of rest, the Sabbath. Some people have the supernatural ability to turn a place into something sacred— by virtue of their presence. They bring everyone into supernatural rest.

The Principle
Fulfillment is "using God's abilities to do what you're designed to do."[59]

The Legitimacy Lie
"I am legitimate when I have earned God's or other people's favor through sacrifice."[60]

This is the opposite of the Sabbath— a day when people completely unplug and simply enjoy God's presence and one another.

The Enemy's Tactic
Ammonite curse (Judges 12), which causes people to reject God's blessings, believing they just exchange something back to God in order to receive (or because they received). Jepthah was chosen by God to lead Israel to victory in battle. He promised God— rashly— that he would sacrifice the first thing to come out of his house if he returned victoriously. After the battle, his daughter was the first to emerge from the home. He kept his vow, offering something to God which He didn't require. The victory had been freely given.[61]

Potential Pitfall
A continual tug of war with God in which we think we just do something to gain His favor. Or, if He does something for us, we assume we owe Him "payback." This can quickly make our faith extremely transactional.

---

[59] *Designed for Fulfillment*, page 122.

[60] *Designed for Fulfillment*, page 122.

[61] *Designed for Fulfillment*, page 125.

The Cross

Luke 23:46, "Father, into Your hands I commit My spirit…"

In effect, Jesus offers Himself completely to God. He does this amidst pain. Many times, people with the gift of mercy tend to withdraw from God when facing a struggle because (when unhealthy) they feel faith is more of an exchange.

The Blessings

John the Apostle. Tradition says he was executed— placed in boiling oil. But, it had no effect. In turn, he was exiled to Patmos. There, he received the vision that became the Book of Revelation. He was also known as the disciple Jesus loved (see John 20:2). That is, he found a place of rest in who he was in relationship to Jesus rather than what he achieved. We must learn to trust God for the fulfillment of our purpose, as an overflow of the relationship.[62]

The Tabernacle

The Mercy Seat is the final element of furniture in the Tabernacle (see Exodus 25:17-22, 37:6-9). The most intimate place in the tent, this is the place where God met His people.

Like the seventh day, everything flows from this rest. Furthermore, this is a seat — denoting that people aren't running around and serving. The work has been done.[63]

The Birthright / Destiny

The Church at Laodocea (Revelation 3:14-22) was said to be wretched, poor, naked, and blind… about the things that matter (even though, historically, they were rich and prosperous). They were encouraged not to seek comfort in the natural, but to rest— to lean into the supernatural. Then, the rest will come. They will be permitted to sit on the throne with Him.[64]

Person to Study

David, Joshua, Ruth, John

---

[62] *Designed for Fulfillment,* page 128.

[63] *Designed for Fulfillment,* page 129.

[64] *Designed for Fulfillment,* pages 130-131.

THE PATH

IDENTITY
DISCOVER WHO GOD UNIQUELY MADE ME TO BE

ALIGNMENT
REORDER MY MOST VALUABLE ASSETS

EMPOWERMENT
TAKE THE PRESENCE WITH ME IN EVERY AREA OF LIFE

ASSIGNMENT
BLESS THE PEOPLE GOD PLACES BEFORE ME

2. Alignment

Main idea: The second step in my transformation is to move into alignment with the Kingdom of God, specifically by leveraging our two most important resources: time and money.

---

1. You have everything you need to live the life God designed; the key isn't to find something "more" but to first set the things you already possess in order.

    A. **The process of transforming an iron bar into a magnet illustrates how life transformation can occur.**

        - The difference between a magnet and an iron bar is simply this: **the molecules in the magnet are aligned, whereas the molecules in the iron bar are not.**

- The result = the iron bar has no power, even though everything is present which is needed for that iron bar to exert tremendous power.

- Peter tells us we— like the iron bar— have everything we need (2 Peter 1:3 ESV):

  His divine power has granted to us all things that pertain to life and godliness, through the knowledge of him who called us to his own glory and excellence.

ALIGNMENT

THE DIFFERENCE BETWEEN A "PLAIN" IRON BAR AND A MAGNET IS NOTHING MORE THAN MOLECULE ALIGNMENT.

THE ALIGNED MOLECULES OF THE MAGNET CREATE ATTRACTION.

A MAGNET CAN "MAGNETIZE" AN IRON BAR— AND SHIFT ITS MOLECULES— IF THE TWO ARE HELD TOGETHER FOR ENOUGH TIME.

B. You can magnetize or re-magnetize an iron bar.

- An iron bar which has lost (or which has never had) magnetic power isn't without hope. **If you place the iron bar against a magnet, the molecules in the iron bar will realign, morphing it into a magnet.**

- The potential— and everything that was needed— was there all along. **It simply needed to be aligned.**

- Remember, Jesus tells us that the Kingdom of God is within you (Luke 17:21). Part of repentance involved "seeing" this, as we learned in chapter 1.

C. Alignment brings the power.

- God gives us the process to align our lives.

- As we realign with His Kingdom, the power begins to flow!

2. The power of "firsts" empowers us to align our lives with God's Kingdom.

A. We all understand the power of "firsts," in general.

- We regularly highlight "firsts."

    - Stores often frame the first dollar they receive. Even though many other dollars come into the store, the first is special.

    - We remember the men who flew the first airplane (The Wright Brothers), but we probably don't know the second.

    - Everyone knows who the first President of the United States was (George Washington), even though most can't name the second (Thomas Jefferson) or the third (John Adams).

    - Many people can name the man who first set foot on the moon (Neil Armstrong) but can't name the man in the Eagle with him, who happened to be the second man on the moon (Buzz Aldrin).

    - As Chuck Pierce writes, "We can all remember our first car, our first date, and our first kiss. The *first* is special!"[65]

- The Scripture reminds us of this same concept— the first matters.

    - Romans 11:16 tell us, "For if the firstfruit *is* holy, the lump *is* also *holy;* and if the root *is* holy, so *are* the branches" (NKJV).

    - The first sets the tone for the rest.

---

[65] See *A Time to Advance*, p85.

B. In the Sermon on the Mount, Jesus clearly tells us to prioritize—that is, to "first"— the Kingdom.

- He says, "Seek first His kingdom and His righteousness" (Matthew 6:33).

- Furthermore, He offers a follow-up promise that if we do this that "all these things will be added to you…"

- In this part of His teaching, He points to the grind of life. Everyone seeks food, clothing… the basics. "For after all these things the Gentiles seek…" (Matthew 6:32).

- Now, it's easy to read this passage and think that Jesus is telling us something like— "Yeah. People in the world are anxious about the stuff of this world…" That is, they are worried about—

  - The things they'll wear. Whether they'll look in style or not. Whether it was made in a sweat shop, or whether a fair wage was paid to the workers.

  - The things they'll eat. Will there be enough to go around? Will it be gluten free? Is it organic or grass fed or does it have carcinogens or other random things that might hurt you in it?

  - Everything else in life. Jobs. The kids' schedule. Traffic. The car.

- In other words, **it's easy to read this passage as if Jesus merely compares what He tells us to seek, as opposed to what most seek.**

- Remarkably, though, **it's not just the "object" of that search which He's suggesting should be different; it's also the manner of "seeking."** You see, the word *seek* in the passage is two different words (in the Greek language) which we've translated the same in English.

  - Jesus says that we should seek "as a hunger, without labor or toil."

  - The Gentiles seek "with much sweat, toil, stress, anxiety."

- We could rephrase what Jesus tells us to do like this: "First, hunger / desire (without labor or toil) for His kingdom and His righteousness… and everything else comes your way, too."

- Notice the difference—

  - The seeking Jesus tells us to do is simply to desire, to trust and act accordingly, and then be prepared to receive— by ordering our lives around the Kingdom.

  - The seeking the world tells us to do is to strive, strain, and hustle.

TWO KINDS OF SEEKING

"Gentiles" seek		Jesus says you seek
WITH MUCH SWEAT, TOIL, STRESS, ANXIETY	VS.	AS A HUNGER- WITHOUT LABOR OR TOIL

- Again, **the contrast isn't just in what we seek, but in how we seek it.**[66]

- We're told to cease striving and rest in His promises.

  - Three times in Scripture we're told that "God opposes the proud but gives grace to the humble" (compare James 4:6, 1 Peter 5:5, Proverbs 3:34). Furthermore, we also read that when we humble ourselves before God, He lifts us up (compare James 4:10 with 1 Peter 5:6):

    Therefore humble yourselves under the mighty hand of God, that He may exalt you in due time.

  - In other words, we could rephrase the concept like this: **If I exalt myself to find my own way, everything flows from me. But, if I lower myself everything all flows down to me.**

---

[66] See Andrew Edwin Jenkins, *Soul Wholeness*, page 352f., for more on "seek."

- It's said that the ocean is the most powerful force of nature on the planet. In some sense, this might be because the ocean is the lowest. Everything flows down to it. The same principle holds true of us when we humble ourselves by aligning with God… first.

C. The Scripture makes this very practical— and shows us how to align how to "seek" the Kingdom.

- Notice what we read Proverbs 3:5-10 (NKJV, emphasis added):

> *5 Trust in the Lord with all your heart,*
> *And **lean not on your own understanding**;*
>
> *6 **In all your ways acknowledge Him**,*
> *And He shall direct your paths.*
>
> *7 Do not be wise in your own eyes;*
> *Fear the Lord and depart from evil.*
>
> *8 It will be health to your flesh,*
> *And strength to your bones.*
>
> *9 **Honor the Lord with your possessions**,*
> *And **with the first fruits of all your increase**;*
>
> *10 So your barns will be filled with plenty,*
> *And your vats will overflow with new wine.*

- **First, we're told to "lean not on our own understanding" (v5).** That is, some things— we're told— might seem counter-intuitive.

  - We also read that we might be tempted to do what seems wise to us (v7), as opposed to the instructions God offers.

  - Notably, we should expect this tension, however, because **repentance— as we learned— involves seeing life from a different perspective.**

- **Second, we're told to acknowledge God "in all our ways" (v6).** The Hebrew word for *ways* here infers the recurrence of something, over and over, as a repeating process.

- In other words, *days* might be a better translation here.

- So, we could say that **we're told to acknowledge God in all of our days, that is, our time.**

- **Third, we read that we should "honor God with our possessions, particularly the first fruits of everything we gain" (v9).**

  - This approach includes a two-fold proposition of stewarding what we have as well as gifting the Lord the first of what we gain.

  - Furthermore, we're promised a result— we're given the two-fold promise that our barns will be full *and* our vats will overflow with new wine (see 3:10).

    - *Barns* refers to our storage containers— which could include everything from our pantry to our bank accounts to our gas tanks and even literal barns.

    - Wine is often a euphemism for the Holy Spirit throughout Scripture (see Ephesians 5:18-19, Acts 2:6-13, Mark 2:22).

  - We're promised, in other words, that we'll not only have all of our needs met but that we'll also experience an ongoing encounter with the presence and power of God.

TOP STRESSORS

THERE NEVER SEEMS TO BE ENOUGH TIME OR MONEY TO DO EVERYTHING REQUIRED.

AND OUR PERCEPTION IS THAT AS ONE GOES UP, THE OTHER GOES DOWN.

- **Proverbs 3:5-10 addresses our most common stressors, time and money.**

  - When one goes up, the other goes down— or so we think.

  - Furthermore, there never seems to be enough of either.

  - Yet we're told that when we acknowledge the Lord first with our time, He orders it. He directs our paths (v6). And, when we honor Him first with our treasure, He multiplies it in such a way that our storehouses remain full and we experience His presence in an ongoing, overflowing way.

- **The promise of Proverbs 3:5-10 (and of seeking the Kingdom first) is that when we align with God's pattern, both of these resources come to us.**

  - Notably, here we are dealing with principles.

  - A principle works in such a way that "man does something and there is a predictable result according to God's prescribed design. God does not have to intervene to make it happen."[67]

---

[67] See *Designed for Fulfillment,* page 39.

- "Many people who have experienced salvation still find their finances, health, relationships, and identity are all in an arena of brokenness."[68] Such scenarios often have to do with the violation of God-ordained principles.

- **For the remainder of this chapter we'll discuss how to seek God first in each of these strategic areas, thereby aligning our lives.**

3.   Time = acknowledging God in all our ways / days.

When we think about "time," we most often think how much of it (or how little of it) we possess. **The Bible doesn't merely speak about time, though; it teaches us about *timing*.**

A major factor related to sowing and reaping— a principle of Scripture we'll discuss in a moment — is *timing*. All farmers understand (and even make plans based on that fact) that different groups grow in different seasons.

Timing is important in other areas of life, too. If you've ever played baseball, you've probably "whiffed it." Your swing may have been *perfect*. But, if you didn't time that swing at the precise moment the ball was crossing the plate… well, it doesn't matter how great the swing is if your timing is off! **It's not just about *what* you do, it's also *when* you do it!**

Chuck Pierce argues that this is spiritually true, as well. "In the earth realm, Satan tries to change times and laws (see Daniel 7:25). Therefore, if our flesh does not submit to God's time, we give access to Satan and that moves us out of time. That is where we start losing our blessings."[69] In this section of the chapter **we want to uncover the timing of the Kingdom so we can experience the full blessings of God!**

Biblical timing occurs when we place God first and when we step into His Kingdom calendar.

A. The Kingdom calendar isn't on your wrist, on your phone, or in your day-planner; God set the Kingdom calendar high in the sky.

---

[68] *Designed for Fulfillment,* page 39.

[69] *A Time to Prosper*, Chuck Pierce and Robert Heidler, pp161.

- Notice a verse from Genesis that you may have overlooked, since it's so familiar (Genesis 1:14, NIV):

  *And God said, "Let there be lights in the vault of the sky to separate the day from the night, and **let them serve as signs to mark sacred times, and days and years."***

- In Jesus' day (and even earlier), people didn't look at a clock to determine what time it was during the day; they looked to the heavens. They didn't look at a calendar to see what month they were in; they looked above them to see which constellations were present in the evening sky. And they knew how far they were into that month based on how much of the moon was reflecting the sun's light amidst those stars.

- **The sun, the moon, and the stars were set in place not only to tell us what time it is but also to show us specific days when God planned to do unique things!** (You may want to review those verses and notice the parts we put in bold print, where God tells us why we mark time.)

- Here's what we'll see over the next few pages:

The Rhythm of the Kingdom

	WHAT	HOW
WEEKLY	Sabbath	Each week, we take a day off and cease from our labor. We create sacred space to enjoy, while our Father continues working on our behalf.
MONTHLY	New Moon	Every month, we see a constellation in the night sky that connects us to a specific event in Scripture. We're reminded of the unique rhythm of that month... and are invited to set our activities to a specific cadence.
ANNUALLY	Three Feasts	Specific times when God ordained to meet His people in a special way. He's literally been celebrating these feasts- and fulfilling them- since the Book of Exodus. There is still a big event He will celebrate with us!

B. The Rhythm of Kingdom time = weekly, monthly, annually

1. Weekly rhythm = the Sabbath

- Most of us feel rushed— as if there's too much to do and not enough hours in the day.

    - We live in a constant state of anxiety— of being "behind."

    - "Even though the twentieth century brought the invention of incredible labor-saving devices, the result has not been a life of leisure. In fact, the pace has escalated greatly... Our labor-saving devices cannot produce a life of rest because **work always expands to fill whatever time is available.**"[70]

    - The truth, though, is that **although there's never enough time to do everything that could be done, there's always more than enough time to do what should be done.** Stepping into alignment with God's weekly rhythm of Sabbath helps us prioritize life by placing Him at the core.

- While giving the Ten Commandments, God paused and recounted the ways in which He blessed His people, God reminded them:

    - He rescued them from slavery in Egypt (Ezekiel 20:10).

    - He gave them statutes so that they might live in honor, freedom, and health (Ezekiel 20:11)

    - He blessed them with the Sabbath (Ezekiel 20:12)

- Notice the third gift on the list: God included the Sabbath in the "short list" of big blessings He had given His people!

- The seventh day of creation was **the first Sabbath, a day that God Himself observed**: "on the seventh day He rested and was refreshed" (31:17 ESV).

- If God took a Sabbath how much more should we?! If God was refreshed, how much more do we need it?!

---

[70] *A Time to Prosper*, Chuck Pierce and Robert Heidler, pp83-84.

- When is the Sabbath?

  - Jews historically celebrated the Sabbath from sundown on Friday evening until sundown on Saturday evening.[71]

  - In this way, **they created a "sanctuary in time."** They set a clear marker as to when the time began, setting it aside as special for them.[72] **In the same way that things can be holy- and even places can be holy— the Jews believed that time could be a holy dimension.**[73]

  - Leviticus 23:25 tells us the Sabbath is a day to avoid the routine work of the week.

    - We don't have to be legalistic about the day— it's more important that we actually set aside a day to enjoy… and to move back into the rhythm of Creation.

    - However, **it's important to clearly mark when your Sabbath starts, as well as when it ends.** During that time, you may have specific things you choose do in order to create sacred space:

      - Abandon social media— and your electronic devices in general

      - Prepare foods easy to cook (or order them)

      - Watch a movie, read a book, go for a hike…

      - Enjoy the rhythm of doing something that isn't work and isn't "productive" according to the standards of the kingdom of this world (but is valuable in the Kingdom of God)

---

[71] Here's an interesting tidbit: at Creation, each day began with rest. Read the account. You'll see the refrain throughout Genesis 1: *"There was evening and then morning…"*

[72] Holy means "uncommon." It's different than the norm. There's something unique and special about it. that's the key for this day. See Leviticus 10:10 and Ezekiel 44:23.

[73] See *A Time to Prosper*, Chuck Pierce and Robert Heidler, p89.

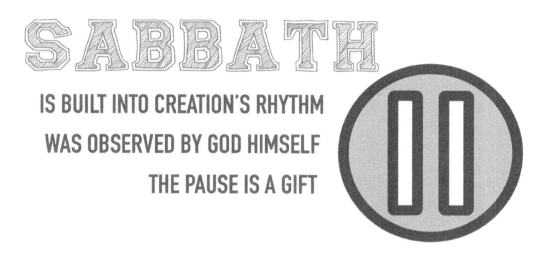

SABBATH

IS BUILT INTO CREATION'S RHYTHM
WAS OBSERVED BY GOD HIMSELF
THE PAUSE IS A GIFT

- Notice, from a religious standpoint, how important the Sabbath is:

    - Bible commentators talk about three different types of laws that God created: Ceremonial Laws, Civil Laws, and Moral Laws.

        1. *Ceremonial Laws* outline how and where worship should be conducted (we read about the sacrificial system here, for instance).

        2. *Civil Laws* note how the nation of Israel was to be run.

        3. *Moral Laws* include the Ten Commandments— which means "it is just as much a violation of God's moral law to work seven days a week as it is to kill, steal, or commit adultery."[74]

    - The Sabbath ranked high on God's "to do" list. It wasn't just an issue of religious observance (Ceremonial Law) or even government (Civil Law), it was part of their moral fabric.

---

[74] *A Time to Prosper*, Chuck Pierce and Robert Heidler, p85.

- The proper perspective matters here, as well:

  - **Jesus reminds us that the Sabbath was made for us (see Mark 2:27)**. The Pharisees created numerous rules as to how people must observe the Sabbath. Jesus "flipped the script" on them and said, in effect, "Yes, this was so important for you that our Heavenly Father made it a rule, but His intention was for you to be blessed instead of stressed by this day off."

  - Moses tells us the same thing: **the Sabbath was made for you.** "You shall keep the Sabbath, because it is holy for you" (Exodus 31:14 ESV). Notice this, though: "It is a sign forever between me and the people of Israel that in six days the Lord made heaven and earth, and on the seventh day He rested and was refreshed" (31:17 ESV).

4. **Monthly rhythm = each month we start anew with the new moon.**

   - Twelve times a year, the moon goes through a complete cycle, orbiting around the earth. **The word *month* actually comes from the word *moon*,** showing the correlation between this astronomical activity and our way of measuring time.

   - Job 9:8-9 tells us (MSG):

     All by himself he stretches out the heavens and strides on the waves of the sea. He designed the Big Dipper and Orion, the Pleiades and Alpha Centauri.

   - **The moon and the stars are God's** (and belong to the Kingdom of God, not the kingdom of this world), including their placement in the sky and when they become visible to us.

     - The moon— and what we see from our position on earth— shows us where we are in relation to each month.

     - The stars highlight which month we're in and what we should expect during that month.

- The chart on the following pages show us the cycle of the moon. Each month begins with a new moon (i.e., invisible moon).[75]

- The stars were given to us, according to Genesis 1:14, to "be for signs and seasons."

  - *Signs* tell us when to expect something— just like the star that led the magi to Jesus.

  - *Seasons* is translated from the Hebrew mo'ed, which means "appointment."[76] **A season isn't just about the leaves changing or the temperature going up or down a few degrees; a season is a time ordained by God.** We'll learn more about this in a few pages when we discuss God's annual calendar and the appointments He has set for us to meet with Him in a unique way.

- In the same way that Satan perverts music, sex, and just about everything, he's perverted a sacred view of the stars.

  - In response, many well-intended Christians have distanced themselves from the night sky.

  - "Satan's plans to pervert the heavens is called *astrology*. It's an attempt to discern the future from the stars… to gain revelation without having to see God and hear His voice!"[77]

  - We shouldn't shy away from the sky; we should allow it to teach us— and show us— the grandeur of God!

- The twelve constellations correspond to the twelve tribes. When we look at them in order we actually see the story of Scripture unfolding in the Heavens!

- Perhaps the chart below helps you see what David meant, in some sense, when He wrote, "The heavens declare the glory of God; the skies proclaim the work of his hands" (Psalm 19:1, NIV).

---

[75] See https://simple.wikipedia.org/wiki/Phases_of_the_Moon, accessed 2022-06-02.

[76] *A Time to Prosper*, Chuck Pierce and Robert Heidler, pp145.

[77] *A Time to Prosper*, Chuck Pierce and Robert Heidler, p145.

Month	Tribe	Constellation	The Story
Nissan (April)	Judah	Aries / Ram	Passover occurs during this month. The ram in the sky reminds us of the sacrifice that was provided for Abraham (Genesis 22:13) and of the promised sacrifice of Christ, who was also crucified during Passover (John 19:14f.). Nissan is the first month, Tishri is the beginning of the year.
Iyar (May)	Issachar	Taurus / Bull	The Children of Israel were set free during Passover. Then, they traveled through the wilderness. God warred for them and demonstrated His strength. His first revelation to them was that He was a healer (Exodus 15:26); His second revelation was that He fights for them (Exodus 17:15).
Sivan (June)	Zebulun	Gemini / Twins	In the third month, they arrived at Sinai (see Exodus 19:1). Over the next few days, God gave them the Ten Commandments, written on two tablets of stone. Thousands of years later, during this time, the Spirit was given at Pentecost (see Acts 2), when the Church gathered to celebrate the giving of the Law.
Tammuz (July)	Reuben	Cancer / Crab	This is the month in which two tragic events happened in Israel's history. While Moses was atop Mount Sinai, the people made a Golden Calf (Exodus 32:1). As well, they were supposed to immediately enter and take their inheritance, but chose to rebel (see Numbers 13-14). Rather than having soft and pliable hearts, they were hardened to the word of God- like the crab's shell.
Av (August)	Simeon	Leo / Lion	This is the month the Children of Israel were originally intended to enter the Promised Land. The Lion of Judah would have roared for them! This is a month to mix the promises of God with faith and receive— the Lion still roars (Amos 3:8).
Elul (September)	Gad	Virgo / Virgin	This is a month when kings historically left their palace and lived in the field. There, they would meet with the people. This is a month when people could be intimate with the king; he was accessible. This is a time, now, when God is accessible- and intimate- with His bride (see Song of Songs 6:3).

Month	Tribe	Constellation	The Story
Tishrei (October)	Ephraim	Libra / Scales	The scales remind us of judgment, which is fitting during this season. The Jews celebrated the Day of Atonement, in which sins were paid for (Leviticus 16:3). This season marks the beginning of the year (Nissan is the first month, yet the year begins in Tishri). Jews began their year with a "clean slate," all of the past washed away.
Cheshvan (November)	Manasseh	Scorpio / Scorpion	The scorpion that's visible in the sky reminded them that, with a clean start, they were destined to reign— just as we are now (Romans 5:17). Indeed, God promised in the Garden that the enemy would be crushed (Genesis 3:15). Jesus told His disciples they would tread on snakes and scorpions (Luke 10:19).
Kislev (December)	Benjamin	Sagittarius / Archer	The archer, a warrior, reminds us that this is a season to fight and contend for what is good. This is the month after the flood, in which God promised we would be at peace with Him (see Genesis 9:13-17). Jews spoke of this month as a time in which things come "full circle." In a sense, as we contend to the finish, we are allowed to begin again. Hannukah happens during this season. We see that even in the midst of chaos there can be rest and peace.
Tevet (January)	Dan	Capricorn / Goat	The goat reminds us to be aware of making wrong alignments as we begin the winter season. Once we have the right steps in order, we can leap like a goat and climb.
Shevat (February)	Asher	Aquarius / Water Carrier	The water carrier reminds us that our roots are being nourished, that life is coming. This month is actually referred to as the "month of trees." We celebrate that the Spring harvest is coming— physically and spiritually. This is a time to plan your legacy and your family's legacy.
Adar (March)	Naphtali	Pisces / Fish	During this month, we celebrate finding supply and provision in the world— often in places that is unseen at first glance. Once, Peter and Jesus needed to pay a temple tax. Jesus sent Peter to catch a fish, and he found the coins they needed inside (Matthew 17:24-27).

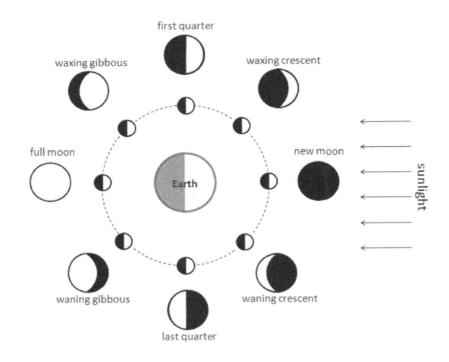

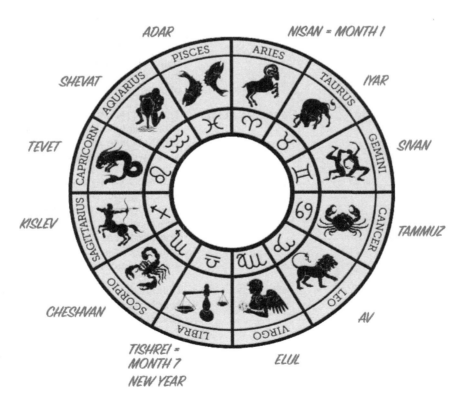

5. **Annual rhythm = three feasts are appointed times (literally, the seasons) of celebration God has placed on the calendar!**

   - Not only does the Kingdom have a weekly rhythm and a monthly rhythm, the Kingdom also has an annual rhythm. God Himself said, "Three times a year you are to celebrate a festival to Me" (Exodus 23:14-17 NKJV).

   - The three feasts are:

      - *Passover—* **a time when we celebrate God's power.**[78] At this feast, we celebrate that God delivered the Children of Israel from slavery in Egypt after the sacrifice of the Passover Lamb— and He delivers us from sin because of the incredible work of Jesus.[79] He cleanses us, as well, making us completely righteous. This celebration begins the Biblical calendar.

      - *Pentecost—* **a time when we celebrate God's provision.**[80] At this feast, we celebrate that God delivered the Hebrew people and then provided lavishly for them, even in the desert. He provided them with His Word at Mount Sinai— and pours forth His Holy Spirit even now.[81]

      - *Tabernacles—* **a time when we celebrate God's presence.**[82] During Tabernacles, Jews make— and live in— temporary shelters (tents) in order to commemorate that their ancestors lived in temporary shelters when they left Egypt on their way to the Promised Land (see Leviticus 23:42-43). They also celebrate that God had a Tabernacle— a massive

---

[78] See Exodus 12:3f. You'll see throughout the Old Testament that one of the first actions people took when true revival happened was they began celebrating Passover again (i.e., 2 Kings 23:21).

[79] Don't miss the parallel of John 1:29, or the fact that Jesus was crucified at the exact time the Passover lambs were being slaughtered that year. Notice, too, how Paul teaches us that Christ is our Passover Lamb in 1 Corinthians 5:7. For more on the parallels here see *A Time to Prosper*, Chuck Pierce and Robert Heidler, pp109f.

[80] See Leviticus 23:15-16, Numbers 28:26-31, and Deuteronomy 16:9-12 for more about Pentecost.

[81] The Spirit fell at Pentecost (Acts 2), which was the time in which Jews were gathered together, celebrating the giving of the Law at Mount Sinai.

[82] See Exodus 23:16f. and Leviticus 23:23f.

tent— built so that He could live among them (Exodus 25:8-9). Today, we celebrate that "the Word became flesh and dwelt [*tabernacled*] among us" (John 1:14).[83] This festival commemorates that even today we journey in a land that is not our home (remember, we're citizens of Heaven!), yet God is with us![84]

* **KAIROS = APPOINTED TIME** = DIFFERENT THAN CHRONOS TIME , THAT IS, JUST THE NORMAL PASSING OF MINUTES AND HOURS AND DAYS... NOT ALL TIME IS CREATED EQUAL.

* **PRIORITIZED TIME** = THERE'S NEVER ENOUGH TIME TO DO EVERYTHING WE COULD DO, BUT ALWAYS MORE THAN ENOUGH TIME TO DO EVERYTHING WE SHOULD DO... PRIORITIZING THE KINGDOM HELPS US SHIFT TIME TO WORK ON OUR BEHALF.

* **RHYTHM** = A CADENCE OF "OFF" AND "ON" IS AS IMPORTANT IN LIFE AS IT IS IN MUSIC. WITHOUT THE RESTS, THERE IS NO MUSIC... JUST NOISE. THE SAME HOLDS TRUE IN LIFE.

C. The entire calendar was created for us.

- A few moments ago, we saw Jesus approached the Sabbath with grace— it was a gift for us! In other words, **time isn't happening *to you*, it's happening *for you.***

- All of the monthly celebrations and feasts are the same way! They are all to be received with grace! In fact, in Colossians 3, Paul says just that (3:15-17, emphasis added):

---

[83] It's likely that Jesus was born during the Feast of Tabernacles. For more on this, see *A Time to Prosper*, Chuck Pierce and Robert Heidler, pp138f. The authors suggest Jesus may have even been placed in a tent!

[84] By the way, Passover pointed to Jesus' death and Pentecost pointed to the giving of the Spirit. The next event, Biblically, to be fulfilled is the marriage supper of the lamb. There's not time to go into detail here, but the marriage tent was a significant part of wedding celebrations. Will Jesus return during the Feast of Tabernacles?

> *Therefore let no one pass judgment on you in questions of food and drink, or with regard to a festival or a new moon or a Sabbath. **These are a shadow of the things to come, but the substance belongs to Christ.***

- Notice, Paul wasn't saying you should not celebrate these times with God. Clearly, with Passover and Pentecost, **God has been keeping His own calendar!** Paul was not arguing against celebrating these times, He was arguing against legalism— against doing them as empty rituals and against judging others for how they choose to celebrate or not celebrate them.

- **By the way, *not all of the feasts have yet culminated!*** The word "feast" is better translated as "rehearsal," as they all anticipated a future event of incredible magnitude, all relating to Jesus (as Colossians 3:17 says above).

  - **Passover**.

    - Rehearsal = The first Passover involved the passover lambs and freedom from slavery.

    - Fulfillment = Jesus fulfilled Passover when He died on the Cross, setting us free from sin!

  - **Pentecost**.

    - Rehearsal = The first Pentecost involved the giving of the Law, a tutor so that people might know how to live in relationship with God (see Galatians 3:24-25).

    - Fulfillment = Now, the Spirit (which Jesus promised) is here, and teaches us— the Spirit which was given at Pentecost!

  - **Tabernacles**.

    - Rehearsal = The first Tabernacles is likely when "the Word became flesh and [tabernacled] among us" (John 1:14).[85]

---

[85] The word *dwelt* in this verse literally means "pitched a tent. In their book *A Time to Prosper*, Chuck Pierce and Robert Heidler make a great case that Jesus was not born in December, but was born during the harvest season. See chapter 11, "Tabernacles: Entering God's Glory."

- Fulfillment = **Will Jesus return during Tabernacles, during the time when the trumpets are blown?**[86]

- In the same way you see God's story threaded through each month, you see the complete story of redemption unfolding in the feasts!

4. Treasure = honoring God with our possessions and the first fruits of our increase.

The Kingdom of God not only has a different calendar, the Kingdom also has a different way of handling currency.

A. The Bible shows us that money is a tool which taps into our destiny.

- Jesus presented money— not the devil— as the chief rival of our allegiance to God (see Matthew 6:24 NKJV):

    No one can serve two masters; for either he will hate the one and love the other, or else he will be loyal to the one and despise the other. You cannot serve God and mammon.

- Jesus said our heart actually follows our treasure. We generally believe the opposite— that we give or spend on things we have a "heart" for. Jesus contends the flow works in the reverse direction (Matthew 6:21 NKJV):

    For where your treasure is, there your heart will be also.

- The love of money is the root cause of many kinds (though not all) evil. Notably, money itself isn't evil— the desire for it is (see 1 Timothy 6:10 NKJV):

    For the love of money is a root of all kinds of evil, for which some have strayed from the faith in their greediness, and pierced themselves through with many sorrows.

---

[86] See 1 Corinthians 15:52.

- Jesus suggested that money (and the desire for things) was one of the three main issues people faced in being fruitful in their walk (the other two being the devil himself, as well as a lack of spiritual depth) (Mark 4:18-19 NKJV):

    Now these are the ones sown among thorns; they are the ones who hear the word, and the cares of this world, the deceitfulness of riches, and the desires for other things entering in choke the word, and it becomes unfruitful.

- As such, repentance in the Bible often manifests itself in how people responded with their money. For instance—

    - When John the Baptist was asked by various group what they should to do outwardly to demonstrate their internal heart transformation, all three answers had to do with money or resources (see Luke 3:10-14 ESV):

        *And **the crowds** asked him, "What then shall we do?"*

        And he answered them, "Whoever has two tunics is to share with him who has none, and whoever has food is to do likewise."

        ***Tax collectors** also came to be baptized and said to him, "Teacher, what shall we do?"*

        And he said to them, "Collect no more than you are authorized to do."

        ***Soldiers** also asked him, "And we, what shall we do?"*

        And he said to them, "Do not extort money from anyone by threats or by false accusation, and be content with your wages."

    - Though not required to do so by Jesus, Zacchaeus responded with the grace of giving at his conversion (Luke 19:8 NKJV):

        Then Zacchaeus stood and said to the Lord, "Look, Lord, I give half of my goods to the poor; and if I have taken anything from anyone by false accusation, I restore fourfold."

- Furthermore, we discover that money is merely a test— if we can use financial resources in a Godly way then we show that we can be trusted with the true riches of the Kingdom (see Luke 16:11 NKJV):

Therefore if you have not been faithful in the unrighteous mammon, who will commit to your trust the true riches?

- The rich young ruler was unable to follow Christ, precisely because he was told to "sell all he had and give it to the poor" (Matthew 16:19-22).[87]

* *CHIEF RIVAL* = JESUS PRESENTED MONEY— NOT THE DEVIL— AS THE CHIEF RIVAL IN OUR PURSUIT OF THE KINGDOM (SEE MATTHEW 6:24)

* *HEART* = OUR HEART FOLLOWS OUR MONEY— NOT THE OTHER WAY AROUND (MATTHEW 6:21)

* *ROOT* = MONEY IS A TOOL THAT CAN BE USED FOR GOOD OR BAD. THE LOVE OF MONEY IS THE ROOT OF ALL KINDS OF EVIL (1 TIMOTHY 6:10).

* *FRUITFULNESS* = IN THE PARABLE OF THE SOWER AND SEEDS, THE WEEDS WERE THE DESIRE FOR RICHES AND "THINGS"— EACH OF WHICH KEPT THE SEED FROM BEING FRUITFUL (SEE MARK 4:19).

* *IS NOT THE TRUE RICHES* = JESUS SUGGESTED HOW WELL WE HANDLE IT ACTUALLY SHOWS HOW MUCH WE CAN BE TRUSTED WITH THE TRUE RICHES OF THE KINGDOM (I.E. ANOINTING, POSITION, INFLUENCE, ETC.) SEE LUKE 16:11

B. Tithing (giving a tenth) is the way we align our money with the Kingdom.

- One of the most well known passages about tithing is found in Malachi 3:10-11 (NKJV):

"Bring all the tithes into the storehouse,
That there may be food in My house,
And try Me now in this,"

---

[87] Tradition suggests John Mark was the rich young ruler in this story— as it was a writing convention for ancient authors to make a "cameo" appearance in their stories. If so, we know he eventually transformed, as he penned the first Gospel to be published, traveled with Barnabas (see Acts 15:36f.), and was summoned by Paul from his deathbed (2 Timothy 4:11).

Says the Lord of hosts,
"If I will not open for you the windows of heaven
And pour out for you such blessing
That there will not be room enough to receive it.

"And I will rebuke the devourer for your sakes,
So that he will not destroy the fruit of your ground,
Nor shall the vine fail to bear fruit for you in the field,"
Says the Lord of hosts.

- Notice the Lord promises two outcomes for tithing:

    - **First, He opens the windows of Heaven** (this remarkably resembles what we read in Proverbs 3:10, about our barns).

    - **Second, He rebukes the devourer.** He not only brings increase, He also protects what we currently possess.

- Notably, this is the one area in Scripture where we're told to test God (see 3:10).

- *Tithe* literally means "tenth," which is the number of testing (10 plagues, 10 commandments, etc.).

- **As well, tithing is not a matter of Law.** John reminds us that "the Law came through Moses" (John 1:17). Some people use the argument that "tithing is Law" to suggest we shouldn't tithe today. Notice the following, though:

    - Before the Law, mankind lived under grace. Paul makes this clear about Abraham's situation— and His redemption (i.e. see Romans 4:13). **Notably, though, Abraham— who lived before the Law— tithed** (Genesis 14:20). Jacob, his grandson, also tithed— and vowed to continue doing so (see Genesis 28:22).

    - **The Law— under Moses— mandated tithing** (see Deuteronomy 12, 14, and 26).

    - **Jesus affirmed tithing** (see Matthew 23:23 and Luke 11:42). Jesus lived under the Law (Galatians 4:4), bringing in an era of grace, which we shift into at the Cross when "It is finished" and the payment for sin has been made (John 19:30).

- **Then, New Testament authors such as Paul endorsed extravagant giving** (see 2 Corinthians 9:6-10), suggesting a tithe might be a great starting point.

- That is, if we live under a "better covenant" which promises "better outcomes," tithing may only be the starting point of something greater.

TITHING ISN'T "LAW"

ABRAHAM = GRACE
GIVES A TENTH IN GENESIS 14.
SEE JACOB IN GENESIS 28

MOSES = LAW
SEE DEUTERONOMY 12, 14, 26,
MALACHI 3:8-10

POST-CROSS = GRACE
EXTRAVAGANT GIVING –
I.E., 2 CORINTHIANS 9:6-10

C. The "kingdom of this world" deals with financial currency; the Kingdom of God deals with sowing and reaping— in every area of life.

1. **The principle of sowing and reaping is foundational to understanding how the Kingdom works.**[88]

- Jesus told a parable about a sower and his seeds in Mark 4:3. The disciples were confused as to what He meant. Afterwards, Jesus shared something enlightening with them. In Mark 4:13 (NKJV) He

---

[88] See chapter 13, "The Law of the Harvest," in *Advance* (Andrew Edwin Jenkins).

asked, "Do you not understand this parable? How then will you understand all the parables?"

- This is such a foundational Kingdom principle that it readily appears in other areas—

  - Galatians 6:7 says, "A man reaps what he sows" (NIV).

  - 2 Corinthians 6:9, "The point is this: whoever sows sparingly will also reap sparingly, and whoever sows bountifully will also reap bountifully."

- Ways we can understand sowing include—

  - Sowing is *not* karma— it's not just "what goes around comes around."

  - Sowing is *not* discipline— though living consistently does bring results.

  - Farmers live by this principle— they know that planting a specific thing yields a specific outcome (which could be confused with karma), and they understand that consistently working is necessary (which could cause us to confuse sowing with discipline). Sowing has a direct link to our activity, but the results are miraculously in God's hand!

2. **You always reap by sowing.**

  - You don't "earn" what you need; instead, you sow for what you need.

  - You plant it by giving it away (in the same way that a farmer plants a seed), that is, by investing it now for the future.

3. **Seed can be of any kind— including financial currency and more!**

  - The concept of reaping and sowing was created on the 3rd day when the power of seed bearing plants were spoken forth by God. **Somehow, we've just assumed that "seed" only works in biology. However, it works in every area of life.** Remember, too, this began before the Fall. So, sowing and reaping is not a result— or curse— of the Fall. **It's a principle of the created order.** It's how God designed life to operate.

- Notice that "reaping and sowing" works in the following areas:

    - **Grace—** people who plant grace and extend mercy to others receive a harvest of it!

        - Proverbs 11:25, "…whoever refreshes others will be refreshed."

        - James 3:18, "Peacemakers who sow in peace reap a harvest of righteousness."

    - **Giving—** people who give generously are entrusted with more resources![89]

        - Luke 6:38, "Give, and it will be given to you. Good measure, pressed down, shaken together, running over, will be put into your lap. For with the measure you use it will be measured back to you."

        - Proverbs 11:24, "One person gives freely, yet gains even more; another withholds unduly, but comes to poverty."

    - **Evil—** people who sow evil… well… it works in this area, too! Eventually, "what goes around comes around."

        - Proverbs 22:8, "Whoever sows injustice will reap calamity, and the rod of his fury will fail."

        - Job 4:8-9, "My experience shows that those who plant trouble and cultivate evil will harvest the same. A breath from God destroys them. They vanish in a blast of his anger."

        - Proverbs 1:31, "…they will eat the fruit of their ways and be filled with the fruit of their schemes."

---

[89] You'll be blown away by Pastor Kent's story of finding himself $18,000 in debt to the IRS. He and Bev consistently made the minimum payment towards that bill for years- all while faithfully giving. As they did, the bill continued to grow, because they weren't even making the interest payments. As the bill topped $100,000 (just a few years later), God led a business man to pay the debt for them. In a night, God accomplished more than they could have on their own- even if they had not given and had, instead, paid the monies they gave to the debt!

- **Good**— we're promised that if we continue doing good, we will reap a harvest of goodness in time. This is why Paul encourages the Church to continue dispensing goodness.

  - Galatians 6:9, "Let's not get tired of doing what is good, for at the right time we will reap a harvest—if we do not give up."

C. Four principles help us understand sowing and reaping.

SOWING & REAPING
WHAT + WHERE + MORE + AFTER

- **You reap *what* you sow.**

  - Farmers understand this to be true. If you plant corn, you'll reap corn- not tomatoes. If you plant squash, you won't harvest bacon.

  - It sounds odd, but many people believe you can sow time and reap money. Or that you can sow money and reap favor with your family. That never works. ***You always reap exactly what you sow.***

- **You reap *where* you sow.**

  - Farmers also know that you reap in the same field where you sowed the seed. You won't sow in this field and reap in the garage. Or in the field two streets over. ***You sow here... you reap here.***

- This works in the Kingdom as well. If you sow somewhere, you'll reap there. This is one of the greatest arguments for sowing into your local church rather than sowing elsewhere.[90] Quite simply, you'll reap where you sow. To leverage the benefits, sow the seed you want and sow it where you want it.

- **You reap *more* than you sow.**

  - The seed is the most important aspect of the process, as it has a compounding effect.

  - Think about it like this:

    - *Would you rather have a seedless apple (yes, they've created them in a lab!) or just one apple seed?*

    - The number of seeds an apple contains depends on the harvest conditions, as well as the species of the apple. However, each seed represents an entire tree- a tree which can bear fruit each year (of more apples, all of which have seeds).

  - In the same way, a seed that is planted (be it finances, an act of kindness, prayer, time, etc.) automatically, naturally generates exponential output.

  - In Luke 6:38, Jesus says (ESV):

    Give, and it will be given to you. Good measure, pressed down, shaken together, running over, will be put into your lap. For with the measure you use it will be measured back to you.

- **You reap *after* you sow.**

  - Farmers know that in order to harvest three months from today, you've got to plant something now.

    - In fact, there's a Chinese proverb that says this: "When's the best time to plant a tree?" The Answer: 50 years ago!

---

[90] We teach that you give the tithe to the local storehouse, where you worship. Give offerings above that where you desire.

- The second best time to sow…? Is today.

- We often want the blessings *now*. Yet, there's always a maturation process for the seed… and it happens while things are, get this, underground and unseen.

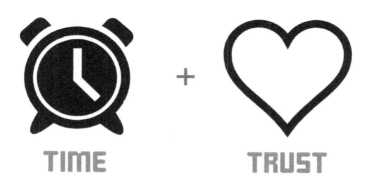

5. Where you are isn't who you are, nor is where you are where you must remain. But where you are is where you must begin.

A. Alignment requires faith. Both time and money require faith, which is action-backed trust:

- Hebrews 11:6 tells us that faith is required in order to live in relationship with God (ESV):

  And without faith it is impossible to please him, for whoever would draw near to God must believe that He exists and that He rewards those who seek him.

- Notice that part of faith includes believing that He rewards the pursuit of alignment.

- Furthermore, faith isn't just intellectual agreement— it's trust that is validated by action.

- And, whereas we don't "give in order to get" (we get in order to give, God flows His resources to us so that He can distribute them through us), one of the many benefits of sowing is that we always reap more than we plant.

B. Alignment, then, entails a front-end investment that is anchored in the principle of firsts.

- Seeds leave your hand and travel into the future.

- Yet they don't remain dormant— something happens in the process of time and trust.

- If you're not "where you want to be" in terms of Kingdom-alignment, just begin where you are. Your identity, as we discussed in the previous lesson, has already been settled. Your identity is based on who you are— and whose you are— not on what you do.

- Alignment doesn't change our identity. Rather, **alignment empowers us to experience the full benefits of the Kingdom.**

C. Jesus Himself is the greatest example of sowing and reaping, by the way. The Father literally sowed the Son in order to, by the power of the Spirit, reap us!

- On Palm Sunday, as the crowds were gathered around Jesus, He told Phillip and Andrew (John 12:24 MSG):

  Listen carefully: Unless a grain of wheat is buried in the ground, dead to the world, it is never any more than a grain of wheat. But if it is buried, it sprouts and reproduces itself many times over.

- The context of this verse is that He's speaking about His death on the Cross, and how He will be glorified in it (see John 12:32-33). **In giving— or sowing — His life, Jesus reaped a harvest of many!**

- As a result, Jesus became the "first fruits" of the Resurrection. Paul says (1 Corinthians 15:20-21 NIV),

  And He is the head of the body, the church; He is the beginning and the firstborn from among the dead, so that in everything He might have the supremacy.

  (Notably, Jesus was raised on the "day of first fruits," that is, the third day after Passover. See Leviticus 23:9-14.)

- This means that He's also the firstborn among the dead (Colossians 1:18 NIV):

  But Christ has indeed been raised from the dead, the firstfruits of those who have fallen asleep. For since death came through a man, the resurrection of the dead comes also through a man."

Transform: Alignment

1. If you would like to review the concepts presented in this lesson again, follow the QR code below to watch the video.

   Use the note space which follows to record any thoughts or ideas you would like to remember.

_____

_____

_____

2. How does the following graphic relate to you and your current situation? Write your thoughts below.

_____

_____

_____

_____

_____

3. In this chapter, we discussed alignment. What shifts do you need to make to experience the reality of the next graphic? Write your response below.

_____

_____

_____

_____

_____

_____

4. A few pages ago, we said, "Although there's never enough time to do everything that could be done, there's always more than enough time to do what should be done."

In what ways is this true of time?

And is it also true of money? How so?

_____

_____

_____

_____

_____

_____

AND BOTH WILL
COME TO YOU!

5. Explain the concepts of sowing and reaping in your own words, including the four truths of this principle.

_____

_____

_____

_____

_____

_____

_____

_____

_____

_____

_____

_____

6. The difference between music and noise includes not only when the instrument is played but when it's not played. That is, the rests are as vital as the times when the notes are hit.[91]

    How does this truth apply to all of life?

    And to the rhythm of Sabbath?

    And what steps can you take now to plan a Sabbath?

    _____

    _____

    _____

    _____

    _____

MUSIC INCLUDES

OFF + ON

PAUSE + PLAY

---

[91] See chapter 19, "Creation's Rhythm," in *Soul Wholeness* (Andrew Edwin Jenkins).

7. Rewrite the following verses about "firsts" in your own words—

   • 1 Corinthians 15:23

   • Romans 11:16

   • Proverbs 3:9-10

   • Matthew 6:33

_____

_____

_____

_____

_____

_____

_____

_____

8. What do you think Amos meant when he pointed to a day when the "reaper would overtake the sower" (see Amos 9:13)?

_____

_____

_____

_____

_____

_____

_____

_____

_____

_____

_____

_____

3. Empowerment

Main idea: I take the values of the Kingdom with me everywhere I go. The church isn't a place; the church is a people. We don't "go to" church, we "go as" the church.

_____

1. This world is not your true home; you're from another time and place.

We simultaneously live in "two worlds," the kingdom of this earth and the Kingdom of God. One is always seen; the other often takes a bit of focus to see. Yet, as we study more you'll notice that the Kingdom of God, though it may appear at first glance to be hidden, is certainly always visible as well. (And, recall, repentance involves seeing things differently— perhaps in a way we've never seen life before.)

A. The Bible declares you are primarily a citizen of Heaven!

- "For our citizenship is in heaven…" (Philippians 3:20 NKJV).

- "These all died in faith, not having received the promises, but having seen them afar off were assured of them, embraced them and confessed that they were strangers and pilgrims on the earth. For those who say such things declare plainly that they seek a homeland" (Hebrews 11:13-14 NKJV).

B. You're also a citizen of earth— here to bless the people among whom you live. Citizenship of the Kingdom and citizenship of the earth aren't at odds (as many Christians suppose).

- We see this clearly in the Old Testament.

  - The prophet Jeremiah found himself in exile, living in a land that didn't worship the One True God. Taken in captivity from Israel, he found himself living in perhaps the most pagan nation of his time.

  - You might think God would remove him from a world with such different values than his own, yet God had a plan for him while he was there (Jeremiah 29:5-7 NKJV):

    Build houses and dwell in them; plant gardens and eat their fruit. Take wives and beget sons and daughters; and take wives for your sons and give your daughters to husbands, so that they may bear sons and daughters—that you may be increased there, and not diminished.

    And seek the peace of the city where I have caused you to be carried away captive, and pray to the Lord for it; for in its peace you will have peace.

  - This is the context of the verse Jeremiah 29:11 ("I know the plans I have for you…"). Followers of God were expected to live their sacred values instead of the values of the world around them. God encourages them to increase in number, and bless others.

- We also see this perspective in the New Testament.[92]

---

[92] Recall, in lesson 1 we learned that to "repent" means to see things differently— from a new perspective. In lesson 1 we also evaluated our identity from a new perspective. Then, in lesson 2 we looked at time and money from a different persecutive. Now, we are going to look at the church through fresh lenses.

- Jesus prayed before facing the Cross (John 17:15-18 NKJV):

    I do not pray that You should take them out of the world, but that You should keep them from the evil one. They are not of the world, just as I am not of the world. Sanctify them by Your truth. Your word is truth. As You sent Me into the world, I also have sent them into the world.

- Notice the balance: **we're destined to be in the world, yet we're not of the world. We're different in order to bless those who are here.**

C. Jesus' message of "repent" was to believe good news and see that the Kingdom was present— that a better way of living is here!

- In lesson 1 we learned that to "repent" means to see things differently— from a new perspective. In lesson 1 we also evaluated our identity from a new perspective. In lesson 2 we looked at resources from a different persecutive.

- Now, we are going to look at the church through fresh lenses. Here, it's important to remember that Jesus said the Kingdom is not only present (Matthew 4:17), but the Kingdom is already within us (Luke 17:21).

2. The culture of the Kingdom is different than this world's.

Sometimes, Christians look at the world in which we live and marvel at how *different* things are "here" than we feel they're supposed to be. If you've ever sensed this, you're on the right track. **The culture of the Kingdom is *supposed* to be different than the "kingdom of this world."**

A. The message of the Kingdom is Good News because the culture of the Kingdom is one of radical honor and extreme grace.

- In the Sermon on the Mount, Jesus contrasts the way in which the world does things with the message of honor implicit in the Kingdom.

- Jesus contrasts two approaches to living.

The Kingdom Culture = Honor

Topic	"You've heard it said..."	Why?
Murder	**Matthew 5:21-26.** "You have heard that it was said to those of old, 'You shall not murder, and whoever murders will be in danger of the judgment.' 22 But I say to you that whoever is angry with his brother without a cause shall be in danger of the judgment. And whoever says to his brother, 'Raca!' shall be in danger of the council. But whoever says, 'You fool!' shall be in danger of hell fire. 23 Therefore if you bring your gift to the altar, and there remember that your brother has something against you, 24 leave your gift there before the altar, and go your way. First be reconciled to your brother, and then come and offer your gift. 25 Agree with your adversary quickly, while you are on the way with him, lest your adversary deliver you to the judge, the judge hand you over to the officer, and you be thrown into prison. 26 Assuredly, I say to you, you will by no means get out of there till you have paid the last penny.	The Kingdom doesn't evaluate actions only- but attitudes. So, we don't look at actually killing someone as much as we evaluate the way in which we honor them. Our relationships- and expressing honor in them- is even more important that our worship. In fact, the way in which we love others *is* an expression of worship. As well, remember that others aren't living by this principle (yet!). So, they may try to "get even" with you if you've "messed up" in the past. Honor them and seek amends quickly.
Adultery	**Matthew 5:27-30.** "You have heard that it was said to those of old, 'You shall not commit adultery.' 28 But I say to you that whoever looks at a woman to lust for her has already committed adultery with her in his heart. 29 If your right eye causes you to sin, pluck it out and cast it from you; for it is more profitable for you that one of your members perish, than for your whole body to be cast into hell. 30 And if your right hand causes you to sin, cut it off and cast it from you; for it is more profitable for you that one of your members perish, than for your whole body to be cast into hell.	Again, we don't look at behaviors only, but at what's transpiring in the heart. So, we don't evaluate if we committed adultery; we go further and evaluate how we're really viewing others… We don't gauge relationships on outward actions only, but by the attitude of the heart… by respect… by honor.
Divorce	**Matthew 5:31-32.** "Furthermore it has been said, 'Whoever divorces his wife, let him give her a certificate of divorce.' 32 But I say to you that whoever divorces his wife for any reason except sexual immorality causes her to commit adultery; and whoever marries a woman who is divorced commits adultery.	In Jesus' day, men could divorce a woman without cause. He upholds the sanctity of the marriage covenant and speaks against "throw away" marriages. Again, the issue is honor.

Topic	"You've heard it said…"	Why?
Oaths	**Matthew 5:33-37.** "Again you have heard that it was said to those of old, 'You shall not swear falsely, but shall perform your oaths to the Lord.' 34 But I say to you, do not swear at all: neither by heaven, for it is God's throne; 35 nor by the earth, for it is His footstool; nor by Jerusalem, for it is the city of the great King. 36 Nor shall you swear by your head, because you cannot make one hair white or black. 37 But let your 'Yes' be 'Yes,' and your 'No,' 'No.' For whatever is more than these is from the evil one.	Citizens of the Kingdom should be so intent on speaking the truth (in love) that they don't have to declare an oath to state, in effect, "Yes, you can trust me, now! I just swore!" We are above this- because we always live with honesty and integrity. Our words are marked by honor.
Retaliation	**Matthew 5:38-42.** "You have heard that it was said, 'An eye for an eye and a tooth for a tooth.' 39 But I tell you not to resist an evil person. But whoever slaps you on your right cheek, turn the other to him also. 40 If anyone wants to sue you and take away your tunic, let him have your cloak also. 41 And whoever compels you to go one mile, go with him two. 42 Give to him who asks you, and from him who wants to borrow from you do not turn away.	We don't worry about getting "even." In fact, we're OK with being wronged. Instead of getting "our way," we would rather walk with honor- even if it means "losing."
Honor	**Matthew 5:43-48.**"You have heard that it was said, 'You shall love your neighbor and hate your enemy.' 44 But I say to you, love your enemies, bless those who curse you, do good to those who hate you, and pray for those who spitefully use you and persecute you, 45 that you may be sons of your Father in heaven; for He makes His sun rise on the evil and on the good, and sends rain on the just and on the unjust. 46 For if you love those who love you, what reward have you? Do not even the tax collectors do the same? 47 And if you greet your brethren only, what do you do more than others? Do not even the tax collectors do so? 48 Therefore you shall be perfect, just as your Father in heaven is perfect.	It's not just our friends and family who are worthy of honor and respect- it's everyone. Even the people who disagree with us. Even the people who hate us. All people are image bearers of God- many of them just don't realize it, yet! Often, treating people with honor actually draws the greatness and glory out of them, causing them to truly come alive!

B. The Power of the Kingdom doesn't come from "fitting in ," it comes from living in such an incredibly different way that everyone stops and takes notice!

- You likely sometimes feel "out of place" in this world.

- That's by God's design. Remember, this world is not your home.

- In another sense, this shows all the more why we need to engage in spiritual community with others who are on the same path. We need the encouragement of others who don't "fit in."

C. Once the Kingdom "takes hold," it begins spreading, working it's way through the entire culture.

- Jesus referenced leaven to provide us an image of the Kingdom in action (Matthew 13:33 NLT):

The Kingdom of Heaven is like the yeast a woman used in making bread. Even though she put only a little yeast in three measures of flour, it permeated every part of the dough.

- A little yeast placed in a batch of dough works its way automatically through the entire batch. It doesn't strain or strive for the transformation to happen. **By its very presence, the nature of everything it touches is affected in a positive way**.[93] This is the nature of the Kingdom!

3. The church is the group of people, the *ekklesia*, whom Jesus calls to live this unique culture of the Kingdom.

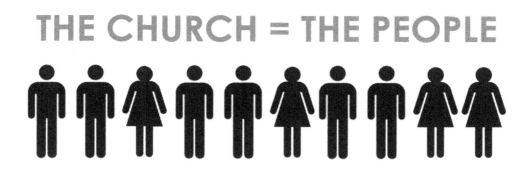

THE CHURCH = THE PEOPLE

(NOT JUST A PLACE, NOT JUST THE PROPERTY)

A. We learn a great deal about the *ekklesia* when and where Jesus founded it.

- *Ekklesia* is the Greek word we translate as "church."

---

[93] Paul uses the idea of leaven in a negative sense in Galatians 5:9: "A little yeast works through the whole batch of dough" (NIV).

- It doesn't mean "a building," however. The word means "called out ones."

- This is different than how we generally use the word. **When Jesus mentioned *ekklesia*, he referred to His people— not a place.**

- The word *ekklesia* was in common usage throughout Rome, and referred to a group of people, an assembly, who came together to help lead the culture, share ideas, and create strategy to infuse the priorities of the homeland throughout their local area.

- Notice this passage from the Matthew 16:13-18 (NIV) where Jesus first refers to His *ekklesia.*

  13 When Jesus came to the region of Caesarea Philippi, he asked his disciples, "Who do people say the Son of Man is?"

  14 They replied, "Some say John the Baptist; others say Elijah; and still others, Jeremiah or one of the prophets."

  15 "But what about you?" he asked. "Who do you say I am?"

  16 Simon Peter answered, "You are the Messiah, the Son of the living God."

  17 Jesus replied, "Blessed are you, Simon son of Jonah, for this was not revealed to you by flesh and blood, but by my Father in heaven. 18 And I tell you that you are Peter, and on this rock I will build my church, and the gates of Hades will not overcome it.

- Notice what happens in this story.

  - **First, Peter receives a revelation of who God is** (v17).

  - **Second, understanding who God is enables Him to better understand who He is.** Jesus clearly gives him a revelation of his true identity, *almost as an overflow of the first revelation* (v18).

    - The name "Simon" means "reed, twig, shifting sand," which is more descriptive of how we see Peter operate throughout the Gospels.

- The name "Peter" means "rock," which is how we encounter Him post-Resurrection, when He begins living from his transformed identity.

- **Third, Peter receives a revelation of what he will do** — he will "live out" his identity and become part of the the group of people, the *ekklesia* Jesus builds (v18b).

B. **Jesus used a common term to demonstrate what He intended to do. He founded an *ekklesia*. Now, we are apostles & ambassadors of the the Kingdom, each one of us carrying the goodness of our King.**

- Paul described it like this (2 Corinthians 5:20 ESV):

  Therefore, we are ambassadors for Christ, God making his appeal through us. We implore you on behalf of Christ, be reconciled to God.

- A few facts about ambassadors that help us understand what this means today:

  - Definition: "a diplomatic agent of the highest rank accredited to a foreign government or sovereign as the resident representative of his or her own government or sovereign or appointed for a special and often temporary diplomatic assignment."[94]

  - An embassy, which is the place an ambassador receives, is a small piece of the sending territory within the receiving land. The embassy is used to generate goodwill, to bridge relational boundaries, and to represent the sending state in the new land.[95]

- Jesus prayed, "Your Kingdom come, Your will be done- on earth as it is in Heaven" (see Matthew 6:10). However, Jesus wants us to move in such alignment with the priorities of the Kingdom, our hearts so aligned to its message, that we can literally say, "My will be done…"

---

[94] https://www.merriam-webster.com/dictionary/ambassador

[95] More at http://olbrychtpalmer.net/2016/04/07/are-embassies-foreign-soil.html

- When Jesus founded His *ekklesia* in Matthew 16:18, He offered us the "keys of the Kingdom" (read: the authority) to serve in His name, on His behalf. Perhaps this is what Jesus meant when He said, "I will do whatever you ask in My name" (John 14:13).

- And He promised that the gates of hades would not prevail.

  - Notably, the original text says the "gates of hades" and not "the gates of hell" (Matthew 16:18).

  - The gates of a city, in the ancient world, were the place of "coming and going," as well as a primary place of business (see Genesis 19:1, Deuteronomy 21:18-21, Ruth 4:1-11, i.e.). Gates not only allow entry or exit, they also exert influence— which is precisely what we saw described in Jeremiah 29:5-7 and John 17:15-18 just a few pages ago.

  - Moreover, although hell refers to a place, hades refers to the personified spirit of hell that exerts influence over people destined for hell.

  - In other words, Jesus said that His *ekklesia* would stand amidst the people of the world, leveraging a greater influence of the Kingdom than the enemy could exert through people he blinds to do his own bidding (see 2 Corinthians 4:4, also).

  - "When Jesus introduced the *ekklesia*, His intention all along was to co-opt an existing secular concept and impregnate it with His Kingdom DNA."[96]

- The location of Jesus' declaration is interesting, as well. Caesarea Philippi, where He founded His *ekklesia*, had a massive cave outside the city walls. Ancients believed the underground tunnels in it led straight to the underworld. In other words, Jesus didn't propose the idea of His *ekklesia* in a temple or synagogue— He founded it at what many believed to be the actual gates of hell.

---

[96] Ed Silvoso, *Ekklesia*, page 23

- By the way, "**Jesus used the word translated *church* in our Bibles only three times (see Matthew 16:18, 18:17).**"[97] Furthermore, He never outlined specific ways to start a church or run a church. And, He never outlined how to do a worship service or most of the things we typically associate with "church." **He must have had something different in mind.**

C. You don't just walk with His influence; you also walk in the authority / empowerment of your King.

- Empowerment is the authority to do something on behalf of a greater agency. For example, a policeman doesn't have the physical ability to stop a vehicle with a raised hand and a whistle, but he's clearly able to do so because of the authority and empowerment of the municipality he serves.

- Authority is more than ability. It carries the empowerment to actually exercise your ability. Sometimes, we refer to this ability as the anointing.

- Jesus empowers us in the same way the Father empowered Him.

  - Jesus said that whenever people saw Him they actually saw the Father. He revealed the Father completely (John 14:7-9).

  - He also said that He sends us in the same way that He was sent: "As the Father sent me, I send you" (John 20:21). This doesn't just mean that "The Father sent Him and He is sending us." Rather, it means "He is sending us *in the same manner* that the Father sent Him."

  - We read that the fullness of the deity dwelled in Jesus (Colossians 1:19). Furthermore, Jesus is in us— with His fullness (Colossians 1:27).

  - It's easy to see, then, that we become an encounter, a connector to the Presence and Power of Christ and all of our Father's Kingdom. *How could we not with everything that He has resourced to us?*

- This is, perhaps, what Paul meant when He wrote about the life of Christ in the believer.

---

[97] See Ed Silvoso, *Ekklesia*, page 22.

- "For me to *live is Christ*" (Philippians 1:21).

- "I... no longer live... *Christ lives in me*" (Galatians 2:20).

- In other words, you are the *same* as Christ on this earth.

  - "As He is, so are we" (1 John 4:17).

  - Think about *light.* We are told to walk in the light, as He is Light (see 1 John 1:7)

    - We read this multiple times in the New Testament— Jesus is Light (see also John 1:7). He even said Himself, "I am the Light of the world" (John 8:12).

    - In like manner, we read that *you* are light (see Ephesians 5:8). In fact, Jesus Himself declared it: "You are the light of the world" (Matthew 5:14).

  - You were originally created in His image and likeness (Genesis 1:26-27).

  - *What part of this has the Cross and Resurrection not resolved?*

- **To encounter you is to encounter Him.** Because of the Cross, the old nature is gone and you have a new nature- His nature. In fact, the Bible tells us that you live His very life... or, that He lives that life through you.

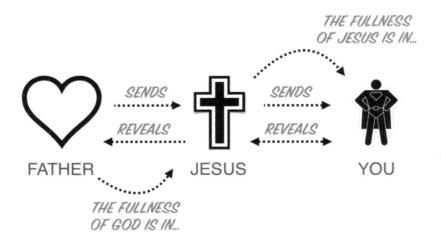

4. Jesus sends us into the world, taking the Kingdom with us wherever we go.

   A. Two commissions highlight our call. Each includes several facets we need to hold together as we flesh out what it means to live as Jesus' *ekklesia*, that is, His empowered people.

Both Commissions Matter

MARK 16:15-20	MATTHEW 28:18-20
The Gospel is preached to all of creation (see Psalm 24:1, Romans 8:22)	Entire nations— not just individuals — are discipled. Entire people groups and regions affected.
Jesus gifts His people with high-level anointing to accomplish the mission.	Jesus also offers His authority— not just the anointing. He insures we can exercise our gifts.
Power. The miracles confirm the message.	Presence. Jesus promises He will always be with us.

1. Mark 16:15-20 is a lesser known but enlightening commission Jesus offers His church.

    •   The text reads (NKJV):

        And He said to them, "Go into all the world and preach the gospel to every creature. He who believes and is baptized will be saved; but he who does not believe will be condemned. And these signs will follow those who believe: In My name they will cast out demons; they will speak with new tongues; they will take up serpents; and if they drink anything deadly, it will by no means hurt them; they will lay hands on the sick, and they will recover."

So then, after the Lord had spoken to them, He was received up into heaven, and sat down at the right hand of God. And they went out and preached everywhere, the Lord working with them and confirming the word through the accompanying signs. Amen.

- In this passage we learn—

  - **The Gospel is to be preached to all of creation.** Whereas we focus on "people" only as God's target of redemption, Mark echoes what David wrote in Psalm 24:1: "The entire earth is the Lord's, as well as the fullness therein." Paul agreed— all of creation is awaiting redemption (Romans 8:22).

  - **Jesus gives us high-level anointing to carry forth His commission.** This includes miracles we don't even see Him perform throughout the Gospels (compare to John 14:12).

  - **The miracles confirm the message—** and are done by Jesus as He works through His people.

2. Matthew 28:18-20 is the most well-known commission. In fact, most Christians refer to the passage as "The Great Commission."

   - The text reads (ESV):

     And Jesus came and said to them, "All authority in heaven and on earth has been given to me. Go therefore and make disciples of all nations, baptizing them in the name of the Father and of the Son and of the Holy Spirit, teaching them to observe all that I have commanded you. And behold, I am with you always, to the end of the age."

   - In this passage we see—

     - **Not only are people discipled, but entire nations are transformed as well.** Some Bible scholars suggest that nations is best translated as "people groups" in the original Greek text. Whatever the case, salvation becomes greater than a mere individual or even an entire family. Transformation affects entire geographic regions.

- **Jesus offers us His authority.** Whereas Mark emphasizes the anointing (supernatural capacity), Matthew emphasizes the authority of Heaven for us to move into our commission.

- **Jesus promises His presence.** He doesn't just promise His power (as Mark emphasizes).

- This is a return to the Creation mandate, a recommissioning of Genesis 1:27-28. This includes jurisdiction over all of life, to reign in life (Romans 5:17).

B. The Early Church— our spiritual forefathers— were known not only for what they believe but for how they behaved.

- Acts 11:26 tells us something that has become common to us but would have been shocking in the first century (NIV):

  The disciples were called Christians first at Antioch.

- This verse reveals much about the nature of the early *ekklesia*.

  - The first Christians were *not* named after their leader (i.e., they weren't called Jesus-ans or Jesus-followers).[98]

  - They were named— by outsiders— after His anointing.

    - Jesus is the *name* of our Savior. His name means "Salvation."

    - Christ is His *title*. It is the Greek equivalent of *Messiah*, which means "anointed one." He is the one set aside by God for the purposes of redemption.

  - Observation: **people in that day saw the followers of Jesus carrying the same power that He carried.** They taught with power,

---

[98] See chapter 5, "Jesus in the World," in *Identity* (Andrew Edwin Jenkins).

they gave graciously, they performed miracles. As such, "outsiders" began labeling them for the same anointing their Master displayed.

- The early church was validated by the miracles that accompanied them.

C. Church wasn't born at Passover (forgiveness), but instead was born at Pentecost (empowerment).

- When we teach only the message of forgiveness, we stop halfway.

- Or, to review the concept in light of the Kingdom calendar we discussed in the previous lesson—

    - Passover = shows us the forgiveness available through Jesus

    - Pentecost = highlights the empowerment that's available by the Holy Spirit

    - Tabernacles = reminds us of our call to intimacy with the Father

- It's helpful for us to remember that the church was born at Pentecost— not Passover, and that the coming of the Holy Spirit (and the subsequent empowerment of the Spirit) is as important as the forgiveness of sins.

THE CHURCH WAS BORN AT PENTECOST, NOT PASSOVER

PASSOVER

THE BLOOD OF THE LAMB
FORGIVENESS OF SINS
PEACE WITH GOD

PENTECOST

THE BAPTISM OF THE SPIRIT
PARTNERSHIP WITH GOD
MANIFEST PRESENCE OF GOD

5. Shift your paradigm. Jesus is present when we gather and He's present when we scatter. He's gives us anointing (ability) and authority (empowerment) to do "church things" as well as "non-church" things.

WHEN JESUS USES THE WORD "CHURCH" HE REFERS TO A PEOPLE NOT A PLACE.

A. **In each of the places Jesus refers to the church (read: *ekklesia*), He envisions a people and not a place, a people and not a property.**

   The Church is not the building; the church is where the people of God— the *ekklesia*— gather.

   - The two places Jesus references His ekklesia are Matthew 16:18— when He says He will build it, as well as Matthew 18:20 (KJV):

> *For where two or three are gathered together in my name, there am I in the midst of them.*

- In this Matthew 18 passage He not only co-opts the term ekklesia, but He references a cultural expression known as the *conventus*:

    > *... when a group of Roman citizens as small as two or three gathered anywhere in the world, it constituted the* conventus *as a local expression of Rome. Even though geography separated them from the capital of the empire and the emperor, their coming together as fellow citizens automatically brought the power and presence of Rome into their midst. This was indeed the Roman* ekklesia *in a microcosm.*[99]

- Moreover, Jesus promises that when these "two or three" come together, that they also—

    - Express the presence of the Kingdom

    - Experience His presence with them

- We saw this same promise in both Mark 16:15-20 and Matthew 28:18-20, the two commissions we just reviewed.

- Whereas Jesus promises to never leave us or forsake us (Hebrews 13:5), and whereas David affirmed there's no where we can go from His presence (Psalm 139:7-12), Jesus is uniquely present when His people gather.

- As we see in the Book of Revelation, He walks among His church (i.e., a gathered group of His people) in a unique way (Revelation 1:11-12,13).[100]

B. Since we're called to live among the culture, thereby infusing it with the values of the Kingdom, we should stop viewing things as "sacred vs secular." Rather, we should evaluate facets of culture as "redeemed vs not-yet-redeemed."

---

[99] *Ekklesia*, pages 25-26.

[100] When we studied identity, we noted that each of the churches in Revelation 2-3 highlight a unique spiritual birthright for the redemptive gifts.

- Jesus is in the process of reconciling everything to Himself (see Colossians 1:20). He is restoring all things (see Acts 3:21).

- This means, practically speaking…

  - **The marketplace and government can be redeemed** (see the parable in Luke 19:19, for instance).

  - **Money is a tool— and God gives us the power to attain it** (Deuteronomy 8:18). We want to continue aligning and re-aligning our resources with His "magnetic pull." (Moreover, the biggest test we face might not be poverty, but abundance.)

  - **Your vocation— your calling— is redeemed.** Paul says our work is worship (see Colossians 3:23). In fact, the root word of *vocation* actual means "calling," inferring that God can place— and ordain— for the members of His *ekklesia* to be stationed anywhere and everywhere in the world.

C. **Our goal isn't to go from "here to there" (Earth to Heaven) but to bring "there to here."**

- **God isn't "for" Christians and against "everyone else."** The truth is that God loves the whole world (John 3:16 NKJV):

  For God so loved the world that He gave His only begotten Son, that whoever believes in Him should not perish but have everlasting life.

- The early Christians wondered why Jesus was taking so long to return to earth for them (the Second Coming). In their mind, it was taking too long. Peter explained that, in God's economy, **the Father extended human history precisely so that more people had a chance to "get in" on His Kingdom agenda** (2 Peter 3:9 AMP):

  The Lord is not slack concerning His promise, as some count slackness, but is long-suffering toward us, not willing that any should perish but that all should come to repentance.

- And, **Jesus encouraged us to pray— not that we would "get out of here" but— that God's Kingdom would manifest.** In the Lord's prayer, He said (Matthew 6:10 AMP):

  Your kingdom come,
  Your will be done
  On earth as it is in heaven.

Transform: Empowerment

1. In lesson 1 we talked about repentance— and it means to "change your perspective" such that you live differently. There, we talked about seeing how we see ourselves differently.

   In lesson 2 we looked at time and money from a different perspective— when we discussed alignment.

   In lesson 3 we took a different look at the church, the *ekklesia*.

   Make note of a few things you learned— new concepts that you hadn't seen before.

   _____

   _____

   _____

   _____

   _____

_____

_____

_____

_____

_____

_____

_____

_____

_____

_____

2. If helpful to you, review the talk on Empowerment. Find it at the site linked here. Then, make any notes you wish to remember.

3. What is the difference in anointing (ability) and empowerment (authority)? And why are both necessary?

_____

_____

_____

_____

_____

_____

4. Is the *ekklesia* empowered to get people to Heaven? Or is it empowered to bring Heaven to earth? And are both needed?

_____

_____

_____

_____

_____

_____

5. Write the commissions from Mark 16:15-20 and Matthew 28:18-20 in your own words. What unique aspects does each author highlight?

_____

_____

_____

_____

_____

_____

_____

_____

_____

_____

_____

_____

6. In this chapter we mentioned the close association between the words *vocation*, *vocal*, and *calling*. Do you feel like you're living part of your purpose in your career (or through an educational or training pursuit that's leading you towards a career)?

_____

_____

_____

_____

_____

Note the following image, then respond to the question on the following page.

"THERE IS A HEBREW WORD, AVODAH, FROM WHICH COME BOTH THE WORDS "WORK" AND "WORSHIP." TO THE HEBREW MAN, HIS THURSDAY MORNING ACTIVITIES WERE JUST AS MUCH AN EXPRESSION OF WORSHIP AS BEING IN THE SYNAGOGUE ON THE SABBATH..."

– Dan Miller, 48 Days

"NOTHING IN SCRIPTURE DEPICTS THE CHRISTIAN LIFE AS DIVIDED INTO SACRED AND SECULAR PARTS. RATHER, IT SHOWS A UNIFIED LIFE, ONE OF WHOLENESS, IN WHICH EVERYTHING WE DO IS SERVICE TO GOD, INCLUDING OUR DAILY WORK, WHATEVER THAT MAY BE."

– Dan Miller, 48 Days

7. How— and why— is it important for Christians to graciously live in the world instead of withdrawing from it?

_____

_____

_____

_____

_____

_____

8. What do you make of the fact Jesus only used the word church three times throughout His ministry? And, in what ways are you experiencing the unique expression of the *conventus* with your group?

_____

_____

_____

_____

_____

_____

_____

_____

_____

_____

_____

_____

9. Finally, notice the graphic at the bottom of this page, which references Romans 12:1-2. Rewrite the verses in your own words— and then record your thoughts of what you're seeing from a renewed mind, thus far, in our study together.

_____

_____

_____

_____

_____

_____

TRANSFORM BY ~~BEHAVING~~ **RENEWING YOUR MIND**

4. Assignment

Main idea: The church exists wherever the people of God go. As such, we take the message of the Kingdom with us. Our assignment is to bless the people we encounter, leaning deeper into the divine connections.

---

1. The New Testament presents a simple way of viewing the main problem people face, and it highlights part of the solution you can become.

   A. **The problem = the "god of this world" blinds the hearts of the unbelieving.**

      - 2 Corinthians 4:4 says it clearly (HCSB):

        In their case, the god of this age has blinded the minds of the unbelievers so they cannot see the light of the gospel of the glory of Christ, who is the image of God.

- Earlier in the manual we presented repentance as "an awakening."

- The Transformation Map below provides us with a helpful tool to gauge where people are in their faith journey— or, to say it another way, their awakening.[101]

  - The numbers on the bottom represent energy vibrations (everything in the world has a frequency— a measure of how alive something is). Though the numbers aren't separated on this chart to scale, they do provide us with a helpful comparison.

  - Notably, only 20% of the people on the planet ever make the transition to COURAGE, noted at 200 MHz.

  - This means that most people live in shame, guilt, fear, or anger. That is, most people aren't experiencing the abundant experience of life Jesus came to provide (see John 10:10).

TRANSFORMATION MAP

| SHAME | GUILT | FEAR | ANGER | COURAGE | GRATITUDE | JOY | ABUNDANCE | PEACE | ENLIGHTENMENT |
| 20 | 30 | 100 | 150 | 200 | 510 | 550 | 575 | 600 | 1000 |

BASED ON VIBRATIONS / LIFE. ONLY 20% OF ALL PEOPLE MAKE IT ABOVE THIS LINE.

---

[101] Source unknown.

B. The solution = you are sent to open their eyes, to show them something better is available.

- During the encounter on the Road to Damascus, Jesus told Paul (Acts 26:17-18):

  *I will rescue you from the people and from the Gentiles. I now send you **to them to open their eyes so they may turn from darkness to light** and from the power of Satan to God, that by faith in Me they may receive forgiveness of sins and a share among those who are sanctified.*

- Paul prayed earnestly that the church— the *ekklesia*— would receive supernatural insight (Ephesians 1:18):

  *... **the eyes of your understanding may be enlightened...***

- Paul said that, we too, help open people's eyes, particularly as we "shine like stars in the universe" (Philippians 2:14-16 NIV):

  *Do everything without complaining or arguing, so that you may become blameless and pure, children of God without fault in a crooked and depraved generation, in which **you shine like stars in the universe** as you hold out the word of life.*

- You are a connector, a conduit, to the Kingdom of God (remember, the Kingdom is within you, per Luke 17:21), meaning that to encounter the presence and power of God people only need to initially interact with you.

  - First, remember what we learned in lesson 2 about alignment; the difference between a magnet and an iron bar is that the molecules in the magnet are aligned.

STEP 1: SEE THE STANDARD

1. YOU SEE GOD'S PATTERN PRESENTED IN SCRIPTURE

- Second, as we align with Kingdom principles (by honoring God with the "first" of our time and money), we become more magnetic.

STEP 2: YOU FIRST ALIGN

1. YOU SEE GOD'S PATTERN PRESENTED IN SCRIPTURE

2. MOVE INTO ALIGNMENT, USING THE PRINCIPLE OF "FIRSTS"

- Third, this enables us to align others, as we step into community with them.

STEP 3: HELP OTHERS ALIGN

1. YOU SEE GOD'S PATTERN PRESENTED IN SCRIPTURE

2. MOVE INTO ALIGNMENT, USING THE PRINCIPLE OF "FIRSTS"

3. OTHERS CONNECT IN RELATIONSHIP WITH YOU— AND, BASED ON YOUR "MAGNETISM" THEY BEGIN TO EXPERIENCE THE SAME BENEFITS.

- Our goal isn't to "win a convert" by telling them to intellectually agree and then pray a prayer with us. Rather, **we want to help move everyone up the scale— just a bit at a time— when we encounter them.** This is a far more do-able strategy and, as you'll see, it's one Jesus used.

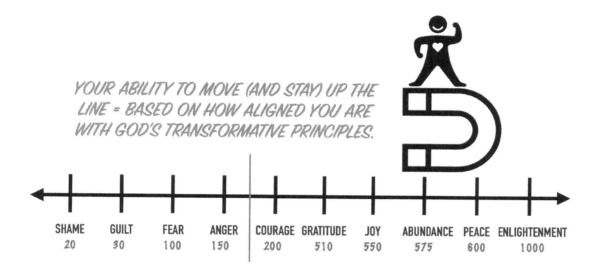

YOUR ABILITY TO MOVE (AND STAY) UP THE LINE = BASED ON HOW ALIGNED YOU ARE WITH GOD'S TRANSFORMATIVE PRINCIPLES.

SHAME	GUILT	FEAR	ANGER	COURAGE	GRATITUDE	JOY	ABUNDANCE	PEACE	ENLIGHTENMENT
20	30	100	150	200	510	550	575	600	1000

C. To implement this strategy, however, we must actively engage people where they are. We must live in close proximity, doing life with them.

- Notice how the early church grew. Luke reports they shared all of life with others (Acts 2:42-47 NKJV):

  And they continued steadfastly in the apostles' doctrine and fellowship, in the breaking of bread, and in prayers. Then fear came upon every soul, and many wonders and signs were done through the apostles. Now all who believed were together, and had all things in common, and sold their possessions and goods, and divided them among all, as anyone had need.

  So continuing daily with one accord in the temple, and breaking bread from house to house, they ate their food with gladness and simplicity of heart, praising God and having favor with all the people. And the Lord added to the church daily those who were being saved.

- Look closely at the passage and notice a few of the characteristics of the first *ekklesia*:

  - They studied doctrine. Somehow, they did this even though they didn't have access to a written copy of the Scripture (many of them would have had the large passages of Scripture memorized).

  - They spent time together (read: fellowship).

  - They ate together and they prayed together.

  - Miracles occurred, just as we learned from Mark 16:15-20 in the previous lesson.

  - They shared their possessions with one another, such that no one lacked anything.

  - They met in the temple (as a large group) and they met in homes (as smaller groups).

- Notice the last item on the list above— they interacted in both larger settings and smaller settings.

  - Over the past several decades the church in America has grown proficient in large meetings. We've learned how to "do music," we've learned about video and production, and we've gotten efficient at moving people in and out of buildings and parking lots. We even gauge the effectiveness of churches based on the large meetings— and how many people come to them.

  - But we've grown weak in the areas of smaller, more intimate gatherings, as well as living out our faith among people who don't yet ascribe to the faith.

- The stats suggest the following:

  - Hundreds of thousands of people will make a profession of faith in a large group worship service at some point this year.

  - Even with the high numbers we see at bigger churches, massive crusades, and stadium revivals, over 98% of people who encounter Christ still do so via a 1:1 encounter with a Christian.

- In other words, we need both the large group and the small group. We need to come together for inspiration, but true transformation occurs when the church is scattered and we all "do life" together.

- In the same way an airplane is unable to fly without both of its wings, so also is the church— the *ekklesia*— unable to move forward to its full destiny without both the gathered and scattered components.

TWO WINGS REQUIRED
or it won't be able
TO FLY

WING 2= SCATTERED

WING 1 = GATHERED

The Early Church gathered in large and in small groups

2. Jesus is our Master and our Mentor; He modeled the strategy for us.

A. Understand the theological shift that occurs with Christ.

- Under the Law, anything unclean (leper, etc.) touches something clean and makes it contaminated (be it another person, an offering, etc.).

- Under grace, the exchange works in the opposite direction. Anything unclean is actually made clean by touching something that is clean (i.e., Jesus touches a leper and makes them clean, an unbelieving spouse is sanctified by a believing spouse in 1 Corinthians 7:13-14).

B. Jesus approached sin as a doctor, not as a judge or jury. And that meant that in the same way a physician is personal, so also was He. Jesus didn't stay disconnected from people— as a judge or jury might. Nor did He deal with them legally. He dealt with the pain-point, the problem at hand.

- Think practically about the environment which surrounded Jesus— and the people who felt comfortable approaching Him.[102]

  - Tax collectors not only felt comfortable talking with Him, they felt confidant enough in His love to invite their wayward friends to a party at which He would be present (Matthew 9:9-13).[103]

  - Women who earned their money in licentious ways knew He would receive them. They were so certain they would be accepted by Him that they barged into dinners where they weren't invited (see Luke 7:36f.).[104]

  - Lepers— people the Law demanded stay away from others— actually approached Jesus so that He might touch them (Mark 1:40f.).[105]

  - Roman soldiers, those who occupied the Jewish areas like warlords, keeping Jesus and His people in physical subservience, were able to look beyond the *Us vs. You* dilemma and approach Him for personal needs (Matthew 8:5f.). Jesus rewarded their great faith.

---

[102] See page 166-167 in *LifeLift*, Andrew Edwin Jenkins.

[103] This episode is interesting, as it's the first time in which we see Jesus dining with "tax collectors and sinners." When asked why He does this, He explains that people who are well don't need a physician- just people who are sick (9:12). And, He calls the Pharisees to exercise mercy, as opposed to sacrifice (see Hosea 6:6, also).

[104] Judas objected to the lavish waste of money on the oils. Think about where the money came from. How does a woman of the street earn enough money to possess a container of oil worth "a year's wages" for a common laborer?

[105] A leper should not have greeted Jesus with, "If You are willing you can make me clean." According to religious tradition and custom, the leper should have cautioned Jesus to stay away from him, because of his ailment.

- People who were considered "unclean" and excluded from the Temple (like the woman with the flow of blood)— and considered to be *so unclean* that they would make others ceremonially unclean by touching them— boldly moved through crowds and *touched* Jesus (Mark 5:25f.).[106] They *knew* they would be embraced.

- Religious leaders approached Him, too. This included men like Jairus, whose daughter was at death's door (Mark 5:22f.). He abandoned protocol and knelt before Jesus publicly, imploring Him to visit her. This group also included men like Nicodemus, one of the elite Pharisees (John 3:1f.).

- As such, the people in Jesus' day made decisive judgments about Him:

  - He was called a glutton and a drunkard (Luke 7:34 NIV):

    The Son of Man came eating and drinking, and you say, "Here is a glutton and a drunkard, a friend of tax collectors and sinners."

  - He was judged to not be a prophet because of how freely He accepted people with such differing values (Luke 7:39 AMP):

    Now when [Simon] the Pharisee who had invited Him saw this, he said to himself, "If this Man were a prophet He would know who and what sort of woman this is who is touching Him, that she is a [notorious] sinner [an outcast, devoted to sin]."

  - Notably, they even said Jesus *ate* with sinners (Luke 15:2 ESV):

    And the Pharisees and the scribes grumbled, saying, "This man receives sinners and eats with them."

- **The fact that Jesus ate with them is powerful.** Today, eating isn't that big of a deal. We'll eat wherever with whomever, whenever. In their culture, though, things were different. Dining together was almost a solemn act. It signified something *more*. It denoted that you were pledging yourselves to one another to live in community. It was an "I've got your back and you've got mine" type of declaration.[107]

---

[106] According to Leviticus 15:25f., this woman *could* have made Jesus "unclean" by touching Him. He would have been unclean until the evening, potentially.

[107] *LifeLift*, page 536.

- Once you know this, it makes sense that…

  - God made a covenant with Abraham regarding the birth of Isaac *as they shared a meal* (see Genesis 18:1f.)

  - The Passover was based *around a meal*— and celebrated every year by reenacting *the same meal* (Exodus 12)

  - Sacrifices in the temple often involved *a meal* the worshiper would eat in the presence of God (see Leviticus 3, 7:11-34)

  - Jesus celebrated the Passover with His disciples, pointing to Himself as the significance *of that meal* (Luke 22:15)

  - Followers of Jesus in the New Testament celebrated communion as a full meal (see 1 Corinthians 11:20f.)

- These covenant ceremonies in the Bible (notice they're all centered around eating) each have a special significance. They're unique moments.

- But *all* eating was important— not just meals that centered around covenant ceremonies. Anytime you ate with anyone you pledged yourself to them in some significant way. In other words, God used a social convention with which people were already extremely familiar to show His allegiance to them.

- That's why the Pharisees often asked, "Why does your teacher *eat* with tax collectors and sinners?"[108]

  - And it's why Jesus didn't answer with, "I'm hungry and they invited me to dinner."

  - Rather, He said, "Those who are well have no need of a physician, but those who are sick." Then— "Go and learn what this means, 'I desire mercy'" (see Matthew 9:11-13 ESV).

  - In other words, "Not only do I *not* feel like I need to dissociate from these shady characters, these are the very people to whom I've come to pledge myself."

---

[108] See Luke 15:2, as well as Mark 2:13-17, for instance.

- Clearly, Jesus wasn't repulsed by sinners. Quite the opposite. He embraced them.

JESUS SPENT MORE TIME AROUND A TABLE THAN HE DID AT THE TEMPLE.

C. Notice the conversion stories in the ministry of Jesus. His encounters seem radically different than what we've come to expect.

- Our typical conversion pattern follows something like this sequence (the numbers are backwards— you'll see why in a moment):

    4. **Believe** = we want people to first confess to intellectual / doctrinal truths we feel are important.

    3. **Become** = when they pray the "sinner's prayer" (which, consequently, doesn't actually appear in Scripture), we pronounce they are transformed— that all things have been made new (see 2 Corinthians 5:17).

    2. **Behave** = we encourage— and expect— them to act in a certain way. Generally, this includes a list of moral obligations that we've put together. And, we may shun them if they don't meet our standards.

    1. **Belong** = we, in time, accept them as one of us.

Typical Pattern

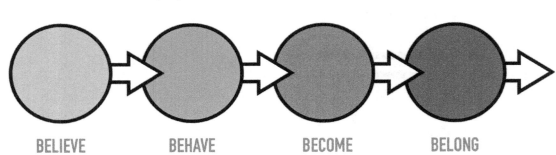

BELIEVE   BEHAVE   BECOME   BELONG

*IN THE CUSTOMARY WAY OF "DOING CHURCH," WE ACCEPT PEOPLE WHO THEOLOGICALLY AGREE (FIRST). THEN WE INSIST THEY ACT A CERTAIN WAY. IN TIME, THEY BECOME PART OF OUR COMMUNITY.

- **The "Jesus Model" works in the exact opposite manner**. See the image on the opposite page.

  1. **Belong** = Jesus embraced people first, accepting them wherever they were on their faith journey. Or, to use language from a few pages ago, He met them wherever they were on the Transformation Map.

  2. **Become** = At this point, they became something different, their behaviors began changing, and they came to believe.

  3. **Behave** = Many made radical changes, even quickly.

  4. **Believe** = The entire process was so organic that, many times, it's difficult to tell when they crossed the line from doubt to belief.

The Jesus Model

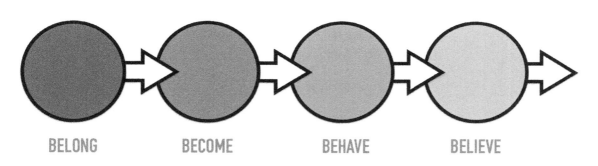

BELONG   BECOME   BEHAVE   BELIEVE

*IN THIS MODEL, WE ACCEPT PEOPLE WHERE THEY ARE. IN TIME, THEY ADOPT THE VALUES OF THE KINGDOM. SOON THEREAFTER, THEY INTELLECTUALLY AFFIRM WHAT THEY'VE COME TO EXPERIENTIALLY KNOW.

3. Everywhere He went, Jesus shifted the spiritual atmosphere. You can too.

   A. A marked changed occurs in the Gospel of Luke.

   - In Luke 9, we read the story of Jesus encountering nine of his disciples who struggle to cast out a demon. In fact, they fail. As He— with Peter, James, and John— come down the mountain and approach the crowd, the father of the demon-possessed boy greets Him (Luke 9:38-42 NKJV):

     Suddenly a man from the multitude cried out, saying, "Teacher, I implore You, look on my son, for he is my only child. And behold, a spirit seizes him, and he suddenly cries out; it convulses him so that he foams at the mouth; and it departs from him with great difficulty, bruising him. So I implored Your disciples to cast it out, but they could not."

     Then Jesus answered and said, "O faithless and perverse generation, how long shall I be with you and bear with you? Bring your son here."

And as he was still coming, the demon threw him down and convulsed him. Then Jesus rebuked the unclean spirit, healed the child, and gave him back to his father.

- In this passage, we see two facts:

  - The disciples failed to do something they were presumably already empowered to do.

  - Jesus appears frustrated.

- In the next chapter, Luke reports that Jesus empowered 70 additional followers, apparently with the same empowerment as the original twelve. When they all gather again to provide a post-ministry report, we read something very different.

  - The disciples report that they were successful (Luke 10:17 NKJV):

    Then the seventy returned with joy, saying, "Lord, even the demons are subject to us in Your name."

  - Jesus isn't frustrated. He rejoices, noting that He sees ultimate victory (Luke 10:18 NLT):

    "Yes," He told them, "I saw Satan fall from heaven like lightning!"

B. Between the two encounters— the moment of failure and frustration as opposed to the moment of success and celebration — Jesus outlines a strategy.

- Namely, He shares the simple framework He's been using all along (Luke 10:5-9 NKJV):

  But whatever house you enter, first say, "Peace to this house."

  And if a son of peace is there, your peace will rest on it; if not, it will return to you.

  And remain in the same house, eating and drinking such things as they give, for the laborer is worthy of his wages.

Do not go from house to house. Whatever city you enter, and they receive you, eat such things as are set before you.

And heal the sick there, and say to them, "The kingdom of God has come near to you."

- Notice that His strategy is based around the table and follows "The Jesus Model" we outlined a few pages ago. It doesn't follow the typical pattern we most often use.

    - He doesn't say, "Invite them to church."

    - Nor does He lead with the question: "If you died tonight would you go to Heaven or to hell?"

    - He doesn't even say, "God has a wonderful plan for your life…"

- Rather, He engages with people on their turf. He takes the Kingdom to them.

UNDERSTANDING YOUR "ASSIGNMENT" CREATES A SHIFT

DISCIPLES FAIL TO CAST OUT ONE DEMON, LUKE 9:38-42

DISCIPLES BEAR MUCH FRUIT + JESUS SEES SATAN FALL (LUKE 10:18)

LUKE 10:5-9 = JESUS OUTLINES THE 4-STEP PLAN

C. Jesus is non-rejectable once people truly see Him for who He truly is.

- The problem (and the reason we often face rejection when presenting the Gospel) is that we struggle to get people to accept a Jesus they've never met.

- Furthermore, we often present Him in inaccurate ways.

- God never sent us to "convert" people but to bless them. In doing so, their eyes (sometimes) open. When they see God intervene in their life, we affirm that the Kingdom has come.

- Notably, even if they reject it, we still know that the Kingdom was near (see Luke 10:10-11 NKJV):

  But whatever city you enter, and they do not receive you, go out into its streets and say, "The very dust of your city which clings to us we wipe off against you. Nevertheless know this, that the kingdom of God has come near you."

4. The 4-step module Jesus outlines = Bless, Fellowship, Minister, Proclaim.

Here, we'll look at step 1, Bless.

A. Bless = the first step in the process.

- Ed Silvoso says, "Bless don't blast." The typical pattern we follow involves "blasting," as there's generally an urgency to secure a conversion.[109]

- Before we talk to people about God, talk to God about people.

- We're told to literally "release peace" to the people we encounter.

---

[109] See *Ekklesia*, pages 215f., for this 4-step strategy.

DISCOVER YOUR ASSIGNMENT

BLESS	FELLOWSHIP	MINISTER	PROCLAIM
LET YOUR LIGHT SHINE TO OTHERS– EVERYWHERE	*GO DEEPER WITH THOSE TO WHOM YOU CONNECT*	*SERVE THEM IN A GREATER CAPACITY AS NEEDS ARISE*	*DECLARE GOD'S PRESENCE & POWER WHEN APPROPRIATE*

B. Your blessing may carry different forms.

- Words carry the power to bless.

  - God instructed Moses to bless the people with His words— and, in doing so, He would be the presence of His name (and the provision that came with His name) upon them (Numbers 6:22-27 NKJV):

    Speak to Aaron and his sons, saying, "This is the way you shall bless the children of Israel. Say to them:

    > *The Lord bless you and keep you;*

    > *The Lord make His face shine upon you,*
    > *And be gracious to you;*

    > *The Lord lift up His countenance upon you,*
    > *And give you peace.*

    So they shall put My name on the children of Israel, and I will bless them."

- The blessing might be a resource, such as an extravagant tip or a gift.

- The blessing might be an action— something you do to serve others.

C. Assess what happens when the blessing is released.

- When you "release your peace" you'll either sense a supernatural connection with the person or you won't. Either way, you have helped the person, possibly nudging them in a positive direction on the Transformation Map.

- If they "reject you," meaning you don't sense a supernatural connection, no problem. This person is not your assignment for this season. Trust that you have blessed them, and that they are someone else's assignment.

- The graphic on the following page highlights what we should do as we bless someone.

  - If we sense a divine connection, we move to the next part of the 4-step framework (the next point in this lesson).

  - If we don't sense a divine connection, we repeat step 1 and bless another person.

- Paul reminds us that we all labor together, each of us playing a part (see 1 Corinthians 3:6-7 NIV):

  I planted the seed, Apollos watered it, but God made it grow. So neither he who plants nor he who waters is anything, but only God, who makes things grow.

- We wrongly think we are supposed to reach everyone.

- Do for one what you wish you could do for everyone.

5. If you sense a supernatural connection and stay (steps 2, 3, 4).

A. Fellowship is the second step.

- Become more involved in their lives. Remember, the Jesus Model presumes connection before conversion.

- And, in Acts 2:42f., we read about the power of breaking bread in homes.

- Suggestion: practice hospitality by inviting people into your home to celebrate *Rosh Chodesh*, that is, the new month. Look in the sky, look at the stories in Scripture, and lean forward with expectancy.

- *What do you do if you didn't sense an invitation to fellowship?*

  - **First, you recognize that this person isn't your "assignment."** You have blessed them— and even nudged them up the transformation scale, so you have honored them.

  - **Second, you trust God to send someone else to bless them and you bless another person** (i.e., repeat the process).

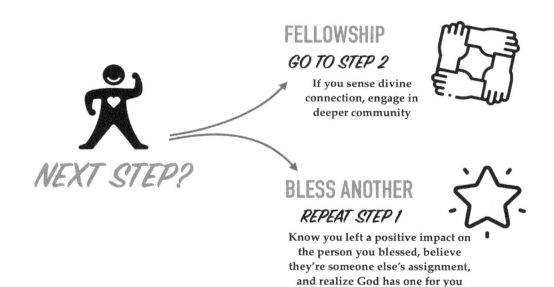

FELLOWSHIP

GO TO STEP 2

If you sense divine connection, engage in deeper community

NEXT STEP?

BLESS ANOTHER

REPEAT STEP 1

Know you left a positive impact on the person you blessed, believe they're someone else's assignment, and realize God has one for you

B. Ministry is the third step.

- God doesn't show you problems in their life in order to judge them. People already feel deflated. God shows you the issues so you can bring help and healing. That is, you become the hands— and voice— of Jesus in that moment.

- Move them forward on the scale…

C. Proclamation is the fourth step.

- When things shift and people ask, "What was that?" declare the Kingdom has come.

- Highlight what God has done for them.

Transform:
Assignment

1. If you would like to review the content for this lesson, watch the talk at the following link.

2. Jesus sent the 12 disciples out (see Luke 9:1f.). Read through Luke 9 and note the issues which arose:

   • They couldn't cast out a demon (Luke 9:37f.), even though they presumably had the power to do so.

   • They argued which one of them was the greatest (Luke 9:43-48), immediately after Jesus told them of His impending departure— as if one of them might be next in line to replace His leadership.

- They rebuked someone who was effectively casting out demons (Luke 9:49-50), when they were unable to do so— indicating there may have been some jealously or territoriality.

- They asked Jesus if they could call fire down on a Samaritan village after the villagers rejected their message (Luke 9:51-56).

In other words, things didn't go well.

But, Jesus called them together and then released 70 more people (see Luke 10:1f.)— presumably with the same anointing (ability) and empowerment (authority) to serve on His behalf.

What do you make of this? What does this show us about the belief Jesus has in us, as well as His patience with our imperfections?

_____

_____

_____

_____

_____

_____

_____

_____

Write the 4-step model we studied in this chapter in your own words.

Step 1 = Bless

_____

_____

_____

_____

Step 2 = Fellowship

_____

_____

_____

Step 3 = Minister

_____

_____

_____

Step 4 = Proclaim

_____

_____

_____

2.   Where are you on the Transformation Map? Why do you score yourself as you do?

_____

_____

_____

TRANSFORMATION MAP

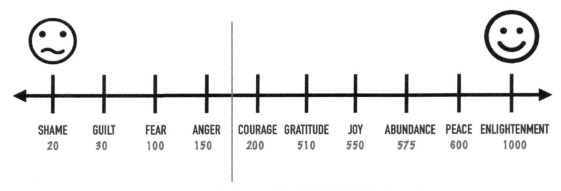

* BASED ON VIBRATIONS / LIFE. ONLY 20%
OF ALL PEOPLE MAKE IT ABOVE THIS LINE.

3. What do you make of the fact that Jesus spent as much— or more— time at the table as He did at the Temple? What does this suggest to you?

_____

_____

_____

_____

4. Who are some of the people Jesus dined with? See Luke 5:27-32, Like 7:36-50, Luke 19:1-9.

_____

_____

_____

_____

_____

_____

5. Evaluate the story of Zacchaeus and his conversion in light of the "Jesus Model" we explored in this chapter (see his story in Luke 19:1-9).

_____

_____

_____

_____

_____

_____

The Jesus Model

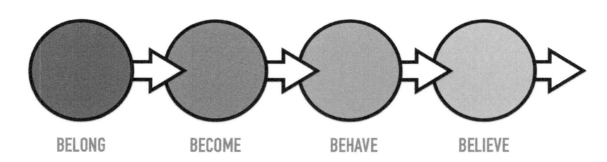

BELONG   BECOME   BEHAVE   BELIEVE

*IN THIS MODEL, WE ACCEPT PEOPLE WHERE THEY ARE. IN TIME, THEY ADOPT THE VALUES OF THE KINGDOM. SOON THEREAFTER, THEY INTELLECTUALLY AFFIRM WHAT THEY'VE COME TO EXPERIENTIALLY KNOW.

6. After the Resurrection, Jesus shared a meal with His disciples to prove He wasn't a ghost (see Luke 24:36-43). Then, He ate with them again days later (John 21:9-13). What, in your mind, is the significance of these stories?

_____

_____

_____

_____

_____

7. The early church— the *ekklesia*— grew through the power of meals (among other elements) (see Acts 2:46-47). Communion was celebrated as a full meal (1 Corinthians 11:17f.). What does this show you about the "power of a meal" as opposed to where churches typically invest their time and energy?

_____

_____

_____

_____

_____

8. The story arch of the Bible culminates with a meal— the marriage supper of the Lamb (See Isaiah 25:6, Revelation 19:6-9).

    _____

    _____

    _____

    _____

    _____

9. List some people you can bless (step 1 of 4). This should include people from work, people from others spheres of influence— such as the gym, school, teams, or hobbies. This might even include people you know from church.

    _____

    _____

    _____

    _____

    _____

10. Pray for each of these people by name— each day for the next week. Ask God to supernaturally connect you at some point (don't be surprised when He does). Record any interactions here, as well as possible next steps (2, 3, 4), as applicable.

_____

_____

_____

_____

_____

_____

_____

_____

_____

_____

_____

_____

11. Remember the process of alignment— as illustrated in the graphic below. Make note of any areas you need to align (full disclosure: alignment is an ongoing process).

Don't wait until you reach "perfection" to reach out to others, however. Remember, Jesus used imperfect disciples with great effectiveness. He'll use you, too.

_____

_____

_____

_____

_____

_____

HELP OTHERS ALIGN

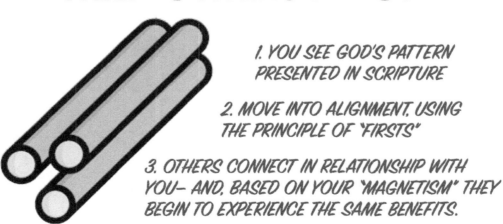

1. YOU SEE GOD'S PATTERN PRESENTED IN SCRIPTURE

2. MOVE INTO ALIGNMENT, USING THE PRINCIPLE OF "FIRSTS"

3. OTHERS CONNECT IN RELATIONSHIP WITH YOU— AND, BASED ON YOUR "MAGNETISM" THEY BEGIN TO EXPERIENCE THE SAME BENEFITS.

Next Steps

Visioneering the Transformation

Visioneering is "the process of making a vision or a dream a reality; building a concept into a workable application."[110] It's a hybrid of two common actions:

- Vision, that is, seeing

- Engineering, or implementing something into actionable form

The icon at the top of this page— and seen on the cover of this manual as well as throughout its pages— is an atom, which is simplistically said to be the building block of all matter. Over the previous four lessons you— the center (read: nucleus) of that atom— have pulled together four ideas: the titles and main ideas for each chapter in the book):

1. **Identity**: My uniqueness is a gift from God Himself. I matter because of who I am, more so than anything I do. The impact I make on the world is an overflow of who I am.

---

[110] https://en.wiktionary.org/wiki/visioneering, accessed 6-17-2022.

2. **Alignment**: The second step in my transformation is to move into alignment with the Kingdom of God, specifically by leveraging our two most important resources: time and money.

3. **Empowerment**: I take the values of the Kingdom with me everywhere I go. The church isn't a place; the church is a people. We don't "go to" church; we "go as" the church.

4. **Assignment**: The church exists wherever the people of God go. As such, we take the message of the Kingdom with us. Our assignment is to bless the people we encounter, leaning deeper into the divine connections.

We initially envisioned these as a path, but in reality each area happens more dynamically than we might see in a linear sequence.

Notice what happens if we use our atom to not only represent you— and your transformation— but we use it to represent people…

Some of these "assignments" might be people at work, people from the gym or sports league… or even people in your church (many people who need a "push" or "pull" up the transformation map are already in your church).

And, some of these people might be people with whom you partner to reach others…

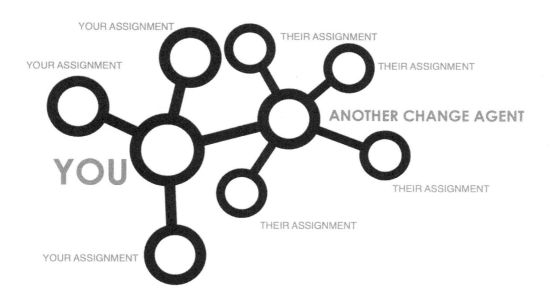

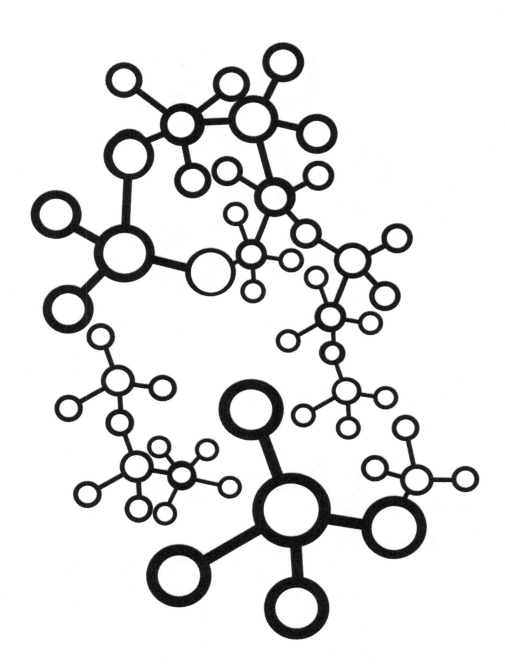

Prayers: Release Curses + Receive Blessings

The prayers referenced in lesson 1 have been included here for quick reference. Note: Copyright 2007, by Charles R. Wale, Jr. All rights reserved.

His prayers, found in the book *Designed for Fulfillment*, are placed here "as is," without edits from his original work.

Note: you can find an overview of each of the gifts at the QR code below— or, link to each specific gift via the QR code on each page.

1. Prophet

Prayer Of Renunciation For The Aramean Curse

Father God, I come before your throne in my blood covenant relationship with Jesus Christ. This covenant gives me specific legal rights. I have a legal right to be free from the enemy's curses and control, to possess my God-given birthright and to reap good things where I have sown good seed. I rejoice that you are the righteous judge of the universe, the Ancient of Days. Open the books in every branch of my family line. Identify every person who has lived in the Aramean curse, every legitimacy lie that they believed, every person who solved a problem that was not theirs, every person who failed to solve a problem that was theirs. Father, cover those events with the blood of the Lord Jesus Christ.

I reject and renounce the legitimacy lie that legitimacy comes from solving problems. I reject and renounce the iniquity of choosing to use occultic power to solve problems. I acknowledge that it was used just for these curses to come into my family line. You were just in allowing the enemy to devour my family line because of those wrong choices.

I have a higher legal right in the blood of Jesus Christ which is sufficient to break the power of those curses. Because of my repentance and renunciation, I receive the cleansing that you have promised in your Word. I send those curses to the cross of Jesus Christ. I nail them there, covered with the blood of Christ. Starting at the cross, I bring that cleansing forward in every branch of my family line, from generation to generation, to the present, to my spouse, to my children and to all my physical and spiritual seed to a thousand generations.

Now because the legal right has been removed through repentance, and the application of the blood of Jesus Christ, I command in the name of Jesus of Nazareth that every devouring demon that used to be empowered by the Aramean curse be gone from me, my family, my spiritual and physical seed, our health, finances, mental capacity, relationships, spiritual birthright and destiny. I command you to go now where Jesus sends you, never to return.

Most High God, build a fortress of righteousness in the place where the stronghold of darkness used to be. Open my eyes to show me how to live in authority, how to grow in authority and how to make the right choices. Release every blessing that has been held back by the curses. Release the financial blessings, the blessings of favor and every blessing that has been accrued in heaven that is necessary for me to possess my birthright. I ask these things because you are a just and holy God. I have tasted your justice in the judgment that has been on me, and I anticipate tasting your justice in the restoration that comes from your hand.

Thank you in advance in the name of Jesus Christ. I worship you for your holiness and for your love. Amen.

Blessing Prayer For Prophet

Prophet, you are a visionary. You are at your finest when you are doing what God created you to do. You try to solve problems through discovering principles and applying them. You are called to see new applications and new ways to implement God's principles in new situations. In many things you are the conception point. You easily do vision-casting to get people, especially leaders, to see the call of God on their life and to embrace pain in order to live in their birthright. You can provide the vision to bring a group of people to possess their birthright. You are fulfilled when you can show a picture of God so real that it takes others to the point of excellence in experiencing all that God can do. I bless this inspirational and transformational quality of your gift.

I bless your passion for excellence in yourself and others, especially leaders. You see the fingerprints of God on the broken and come alongside them to restore. You celebrate who the person can become when liberated from their bondage. Your passion for restoration draws you to brokenness, as you see the evil of sin and the restorative power of God. You understand the deep damage done to people and to the kingdom when sin is dealt with lightly. You stand in the gap between what is and what could be. You are quick to say this is wrong, but you know how to wisely handle principles of grace, reconciliation and rebuilding to restore a broken life.

I bless your fierce intentionality and intensity. Let God sanctify that gift of excellence because He is excellent, so that you don't fall into perfectionism. I bless your need to be alone. God wants time alone with you for intimacy with Him. It is important to give Him this first-fruits of your time.

It seems that you are called to pay a higher price than other gifts in your personal disciplines. There are seasons when God seems to be silent in your life. I bless you during these pruning times to build a deeper root system for greater productivity in fruit that remains. In these times God is drawing you up to a higher level. I bless you with making sense of your wilderness experiences, but sometimes you can see it only in hindsight.

I bless your commitment to abstract truth. You demonstrate faith based on the principles of God's Word. "God said it. I believe it. This truth will work. Let's go with it." The fear of the Lord is your stock-in-trade. I bless you with keen, sensitive ears to what God desires, because when you hear from Him you will do it. You often stand like a signpost directing toward the Way, the Truth and the Life to incite others to action, to turn their eyes toward God, and to urge them forward.

You take initiative and enjoy new things. You shift gears quickly, and you change from one direction to another. You are active, not passive. Independence is a high value. You are a trail blazer and pioneer, not a city-dweller. You are a catalyst, not a slow responder. You think outside the box. You hate maintaining the status quo. You know no fear in your basic boldness. You are not intimidated by the unknown or change. I bless your hard work, your persistence, endurance, and "keep on keeping on" when others would quit. I bless your doing the right thing at great personal cost because it is the right thing to do. I bless your need to have a goal, a reason to live and an objective. You cannot tolerate having no options. You do not like to be locked into one plan that is not allowed to be improved or changed. You want to make sense out of everything, even unreasonable situations. You don't do well when there is no reason, no point, no progress toward a positive end. You need the "why". I bless you to let God be God at times when He does not choose to tell you the "why".

I bless you to learn to establish appropriate bridges in relationship without compromising truth, in order to get truth accepted by relational people. I bless you with patience in earning the right to speak because of relationship, when you believe that truth speaks for itself. As you are willing to embrace relationship, you will speak as God wants you to speak into situations.

You tend to see things in black and white, right and wrong. You hate lukewarm, mediocre and compromise. I bless that intolerance for mediocrity and shades of gray. Let God temper it with viewing others through the blood of Jesus, who was full of grace and truth. I bless you with the fullness of grace to see beyond "win-lose" to seek out "win-win" responses and solutions.

I bless your compulsion for honesty, vulnerability, integrity and transparency. You are verbally expressive and articulate, often the first to speak in a group. You recoil from hidden agendas, manipulation and deception. You have keen discernment to quickly assess and evaluate people and situations. You can spot rebels and phonies, especially in leadership. Your first impression is right nine times out of ten. You do not tolerate rebellion, hypocrisy and denial. You process quickly and have an opinion on everything. Give that discernment to God and ask Him what He wants to do with it. I bless you to let God add his measure of grace so that your discernment does not turn to judgment, criticism and bitterness.

You can build, not just criticize. You can identify a problem, embrace it and apply the right principle to effectively make things right. You always seek right solutions. I bless your God-given sense of justice to be a champion for people to receive everything that God wants them to have.

You tend to be hard on yourself and are prone to self-condemnation. Your default position is that you messed up, or didn't do enough or didn't do it right. I bless you with taking your failures or shortcomings to the throne of grace and there to find mercy in the face of your Father.

I bless your wide range of emotions. You are intense and passionate. Jesus was the essence of joy, but He was called a man of sorrows. He spoke with passionate urgency, pity and anger about religious life in his day. You can experience depression but are also one of the best at celebrating what God has done.

I bless your generosity and loyalty. I bless you with God's wisdom in giving and bestowing loyalty. I bless you with growth in grace in your major battlefields-- alienation, unforgiveness and bitterness. I bless you to come into alignment with God's purposes, so that there is less struggle between spirit, soul and body. You are the first-fruits of God's gifts, and I bless you with maturing into God's beautiful full intention. Let Him call the expression of your gift up higher into all that He sees when He looks at you. I bless with you with gaining from the Spirit of God a new understanding of who you are as God designed you to be. I bless you in Jesus' name. Amen.

2. Servant

Prayer Of Renunciation Of The Moabite Curse

Father God, you are the God of seasons. There is a season for nurture and a season to be the nurturer. There is a season for childhood and a season for adulthood. I rejoice in the authority and responsibility that you have given to parents and others in positions of leadership. The proper order of life is for those in authority to build a platform for the success of those under their authority, and to release them at the proper time.

Open the books in my generational line, and identify every event where an authority figure in my family line, or over my family line, failed to release those who should have been released. Father, this is contrary to your design. Identify every instance where somebody under authority chose to embrace family peace at the expense of possessing their birthright. That is sin, and I reject and renounce it. Identify every incident where somebody took their freedom wrongly in order to possess their birthright. That is sin. Cover these three classes of sins with the blood of the Lord Jesus Christ.

It was just and right for the Moabite curse to be in my family line because people violated your law, but the righteous law of liberty is greater than the law of sin and death. I stand in the cleansing of the cross of Jesus. I command every devouring spirit that once was empowered by the sins that are now under the blood to leave me, my spouse and my physical and spiritual seed to a thousand generations and not to return. Ancient of Days, as the righteous Judge of the universe, enforce your righteous decrees.

Enlarge my boundaries to give me freedom of movement to accomplish everything you have designed for me to accomplish. If I need to leave, give me clear direction about how to do that in a way that you will bless and that will not empower the enemy. In accordance with your Word, release that generational blessing of peace and open borders to my spiritual and physical seed. Thank you by faith in advance in the name of the Lord Jesus Christ. Amen.

Blessing Prayer For Servant

I bless you for the richness you bring to life in caring for the needs of others in practical ways. You know the blessedness of giving of yourself in acts of kindness, thoughtfulness and "second-mile" effort for others. You preach sermons without words, with sermons of service. You have few enemies. I bless your way of love and grace that puts people at ease. You communicate that the purpose of life is people. You are a good listener. You are genuine and personal in relationships. You see the best in others.

I bless your desire to invest your life daily, moment by moment, in things that last. But because of your desire to meet needs and please people, you have difficulty saying "no" to competing demands. You can get overcommitted when you default to meeting people's needs without asking God. I bless you with learning the art of knowing when to serve. God wants to define who you are and help you empower others with responsibility, not enable them. Be free in the Spirit to say a holy righteous "no", even to some good things, in order to say "yes" to God's best.

I bless you for being totally trustworthy and working very hard. You exemplify a life well lived. Nothing higher can be said than that you love, live for and give yourself to the right things.

Your strong sense of responsibility tends to attract people who hold their rights and a sense of entitlement. You tend to be exploited by those looking for an enabler, calling others to grow in character is more important than meeting their immediate needs. I bless you to present your entire being available to God for his purposes, not the agenda of others.

Satan's only defense against the authority and anointing of your servant gift is to get you to believe the lie that you are nobody. Therefore, you tend to have a battle for self-worth. You may have attracted dishonor, especially in the home. I bless you to see the value in yourself, and believe God's truth about yourself and your call. Let Jesus impart to your spirit true statements about the honor you are due. I bless you with a download from God of personal identity, worth, dignity and legitimacy that conquers shame, dishonor and victimization. I bless you with knowing the honor you have as one who carries the name of Jesus. Your shield of honor is the cross of Jesus. Receive the affirmation of others without finding something to apologize for. Choose to be seen as competent and excellent as you are. God wants people to see who you are as a reflection of His Son Jesus. You are you, and you are beautiful. I bless you to live in humility and love, rejecting dishonor and receiving the honor that Jesus thinks is due you.

I bless you because you see the best in others when no one else does. You minister to the hardest cases, the ones everybody else gives up on. You treat everybody as if you are entertaining angels unawares. You see in a person, whom others have discarded, the potential for that person to be transformed by God and to be life-giving in their world. You embrace the deeply wounded through their pain. You demonstrate that God is a God of second chances.

I bless the purity of your motives. You can be trusted and are straight-forward, possessing integrity, truthfulness and honesty. I honor you for your qualities of purity of heart.

I bless your loyalty to your family. I bless you with God's purpose, desire and focus as you minister to them. Ask him to shine his truth on their true needs and your place in meeting them. I bless you to have the mind of Christ and healthy boundaries to provide a safe place for people to find their birthright; without rescuing them or falling into a savior mentality. I bless your passion for family, family restoration, marriage and parent/child relationships. You have authority in prayer to bring the extended family to restoration. Rise up into new authority for specific restoration in people and generational restoration in families--salvation, deliverance, wholeness.

I bless your anointing to bring people back to joy, but you can become a burden-bearer with worry, anxiety and false responsibility if you take on other people's problems. You are a joy-giver, but you are not responsible for the happiness of others.

You are a team player who likes clear parameters and guidelines. I bless your lack of desire to build your own kingdom. You work well with others. You are jealous for God's honor, and your heart motive is to advance the kingdom of God regardless of the expense to self. It is right for you to not prefer the spotlight. You don't pursue fame or steal God's glory, but ask God to remove from you the label of invisibility. You are irreplaceable and vital to the life of all the gifts and in the body of Christ and the world.

Many leaders have servants around them. You are drawn to leaders and those in authority. You desire to make them successful. You have authority to pray for leaders in all areas. You have great fulfillment in knowing you are a life-giver to those you serve. You desire to empower others to achieve their best. You have a long history of building a platform under others. You have great spiritual authority in prayer to pray for most of the authority structures that God established - marriage, parenting, church, government and business. God uses your desire for invisibility positively and lets you go into many places under the radar for his prayer assignments.

You are drawn to pray for government. I bless your anointing to pray for governmental authority. When you live in your authority and pray for the life of God to flow into government, God intends that you see measurable results in transformation on spiritual and social issues.

I bless your desire to pray for life-and-death situations. You are tenacious in not accepting death as the answer. I bless your authority to pray, especially about premature death in leaders, family, captives and wounded ones.

You have a particular stewardship in prayer for healing the ecology and cleansing land, air and water. I bless your authority for the restoration of the environment that has been damaged by the sin of man. You recognize defilement in land and apply the laws of repentance and cleansing. You intuitively bless land in alignment with the purposes of God in creation. Be bold in prayer to put a heavenly stamp on God's purposes in the earth.

I bless you with being mighty in spirit with wisdom, gentleness and dignity. I affirm your resilience of spirit, as your spirit partners with the Holy Spirit for victory and secure boundaries to operate in peace. Your focal point is God's kingdom of righteousness, peace and joy in the Holy Spirit. I bless you with quietness and stillness inside and total assurance.

I bless you with seeing more reconciliation, more deliverance, healing and miracles - signs of God's favor and presence on you - as you move with Him in the power of purity in the purifying mantle of the servant. Your glorious release has begun by God's goodness and unmerited grace. I bless you in Jesus' name. Amen.

3. Teacher

Prayer Of Renunciation Of The Philistine Curse

Almighty God and heavenly Father, the earth is yours. You created it, and you designed it to be under your dominion. You called man to live in dominion and to keep the earth under the kingship of Jesus Christ. I confess that I, and my family, have failed miserably. We have enthroned the enemy on your land and in our lives. I reject and renounce the sins that opened the door for the Philistine curse. I reject the fear of man that has caused me, and some of my forefathers, to not obey truth because of fear of offending someone. I confess this as iniquity, and repudiate that cowardice. I, and some of my forefathers, have used knowledge of truth as a basis for personal legitimacy. That is iniquity. I, and some of my forefathers, have used truth to bring people into bondage. I have attempted to control through truth. That is wrong. The truth was designed to set people free. It is not to be used to bring people into bondage to human institutions.

Open the books at every point in my family line where this iniquity has come in. It was just and right for the Philistine curse to come into my family line because of these iniquities. I appeal to the greater source of justice and righteousness, the death of the Lord Jesus Christ and his finished work on the cross; which is more than enough to blot out every sin and iniquity my forefathers committed. Apply the blood of Christ to blot out these iniquities. Based on the word of my testimony, the blood of the Lamb and the promises in your Word, I appropriate cleansing now. I command every demonic structure that has been established in my life or my ministry to be torn down in the name of Jesus. I command this blocking, devouring spirit to leave my family, my physical and spiritual seed to a thousand generations. Consume with your fire all evil dominion that enthroning the enemy has left in our family line. Restore the years that the locusts have eaten. Restore the blessings that should have been mine that were robbed from me because of this curse. Especially restore godly covenant relationships so that I can be a person of destiny.

Teach me how to live in the opposite spirit. Give me your strategies for possessing the land, for possessing my birthright and the resources needed to accomplish your will.

You alone know what is necessary in my life. Speak the truth, and give me the grace to live out that truth no matter how strange it appears. You are welcome in my life. I transfer ownership of all that I am, and all that I have to Jesus Christ. I bend my knee and proclaim him King over my life. I do this in the presence of earthly witnesses, the angelic realms and the demons themselves. Lord Jesus Christ, release your godly dominion over all that I am, and all that I have. Amen.

Blessing Prayer For Teacher

I bless your God-given need to validate truth. It is central to who you are. You serve the body of Christ when you look at things from a number of different angles to validate truth. This is one of the best ways to identify the teacher gift (Luke 1:1-4). Luke, with his teacher gift, wrote more details on the history of the early church than any other New Testament author.

You have a hunger for understanding that causes you to ask many questions. I bless you to celebrate the power and presence of God, seeing his fingerprints and rejoicing over what He is doing. I bless you to incarnate the person and character of Jesus, not just document Him. Resist the temptation to verify truth with your natural wisdom and rely on your knowledge, intellect or education. I bless you to cultivate relationship with Jesus, see Him in the Word and to know Him, not just know about Him. (John 5:39-40; Jeremiah 9:23)

I honor you for your commitment to go to the Word of God first. The best reflection of God's truth is incarnated in your life, not in discussions, arguments, words or ideas. I bless you to take care of your own spirit, so that you can speak into the emptiness of others and share truth relevantly and persuasively.

I bless your gift that causes you to be careful and precise in sharing details, like Luke. Luke 3:1 is a snapshot of the detailed and historically accurate mindset of a teacher. I bless you to move in the strength of your gift and to mine the goldmine of your gift.

You prefer the old, established and validated because the tried-and-true is more credible to you. You make others stop and consider things biblically. You are not easily swayed from the truth, an anchor against every wind of doctrine. We need your anchor to the Word to not spin off after every religious fad. We need you to systematically organize and present truth, yet make going forward in God the point of reference for all choices, not defending what was. I bless you with a new word in your vocabulary... "yet". We've never done it that way... yet.

Some teachers look for more credentials or more degrees to attest to their competence. This is man's validation and legitimizing. Identity is the issue. When that is settled in Christ, you understand who you are, and you know your purpose. Then you can step up into leadership without further validation from man. I bless you with hearing and knowing who you are and what your Father designed you to do.

You process and make decisions slowly. In your search for truth, find the true wisdom of trusting God when you can't figure things out. One of your strengths is that you do not reject new ideas outright, but you do not go forward as quickly as visionaries think you ought to. Repeatedly Scripture says of Mary, "She pondered all these things in her heart." Give your spirit the space, the time and the solitude it needs.

I bless the way God designed you. God made you the way you are, and He likes you the way you are. God did not make a mistake when he designed you. You listen, observe, gather all the evidence, process everything and summarize it in your mind. Then you give one or two sentences that summarizes and clarifies the whole picture. God made you to slow down impulsive people who jump to conclusions too quickly. The synergy of the prophet, teacher and mercy can be huge when you work together bringing your strengths to bear. Prophet presents truth and brings to conviction, teacher is ready to point the way back to reconciliation and mercy brings healing and cleansing into alignment.

I bless you as God challenges your faith, when you want to know the outcome before beginning. You may not be willing to begin a process until you can see the end. God gives the next step, and He expects you to obey that before He reveals what comes next. I bless you to not let fear immobilize you and keep you from obeying God.

You are deeply committed to leadership. Samuel's loyalty to Saul exemplifies this. God removed Saul and his family line from his position as king because of his iniquity, yet Samuel grieved for him. Likewise Luke was loyal to Paul to the end when Demos, Crescens, Titus, and others went off in different directions. I bless your deep loyalty to leaders.

You tend to have a wonderful sense of humor and can defuse a volatile discussion with a quick, charming one-liner. You are a safe person emotionally, and wounded people feel comfortable being around you. You can listen to brokenness and sin without a critical attitude. You will not reject a person in sin, and will lay out a path of obedience for him and let him choose. You are great at holding the standard of righteousness and making the way of reconciliation after there has been a violation of the standard. Isaiah modeled this in Isaiah 1:1-15. This is classic teacher. I bless your priestly strength and calling of presenting people to God and representing God to people with blessing.

Intimacy and prayer can be a battleground for you. Pursue intimacy with God at the very highest level. Don't settle for knowledge and miss intimacy with God in in-depth personal interaction with Him. You have the duality of validating truth and experiencing intimate relationship with Him. Live in intimacy and worship by feeding both your spirit and your mind. Cultivate listening to both the Word and the Spirit speaking to you and encouraging you. It's the best of both worlds-- spirit and truth.

I bless you teacher, to reveal Jesus as He is. I bless you to come forth with righteousness, refreshment, refuge, redemption, restoration, reconciliation and resurrection. This is your time to show the world the Lord Jesus Christ who reveals the Father, to have that kind of intimate personal relationship.

Responsibility is the key issue for the teacher. You tend to be unwilling to impose responsibility on others, and have difficulty compelling others to do what is right. You do not like to take the initiative to confront that which is wrong. You wait for the sinner to become convicted and come for help. This is a strength, but it can also be a weakness if you are too tolerant of sin, too patient with people who are doing wrong. It is appropriate to give people time to repent.

We thank God for your gift. There is a time for showing kindness, but there is a time for confronting. When God says, "Enough!" I bless you with sensitivity to His voice. I bless you to be filled with wisdom, understanding, counsel, knowledge, fear of the Lord and wise God-centered confrontation when necessary in the right time.

I bless you in areas where you excel in responsibility, and I bless you to not to compartmentalize responsibility. I bless your responsibility and stewardship across the board which the Father has entrusted to you, particularly at home. I bless you to develop the discipline necessary to support your giftedness.

I bless you to be a son, not a slave. I bless your sons to be taught of the Lord, and great will be their peace. I bless you to fulfill your gifting in your generation so that life and healing are released for succeeding generations. I bless your generational nurturing of your sons and daughters--physical and spiritual—in the training and reverence of the Lord, so that generational blessings will pursue subsequent generations. I bless this time of your birthright with all the timeliness of Ecclesiastes 3:1-11. I ask God to give you significant authority in the blessing of Daniel, where you have the information that you need in a timely manner for strategic options, as you are committed to using the truth to set people free. Prepare the way of the Lord in righteous alignment with His purposes and His time. I bless you with great anticipation, great joy, great peace, great hope and great fulfillment in Jesus' name. Amen.

4. Exhorter

Prayer Of Renunciation Of The Canaanite Curse

Almighty God and heavenly Father, you are the source of life and the source of authority. In you, life and authority meet. You are absolute authority, and yet it is utterly life-giving. I acknowledge that I have not lived in life-giving authority. Open the books of my life and of my forefathers in my family line.

I reject and renounce the belief that legitimacy can be established through popularity. I confess that I and some of my forefathers have lived in that belief. I reject that lie. I reject and renounce the spirit of denial that refuses to recognize the reproofs of life. I reject and renounce shifting the consequences of my bad choices to others. I reject and renounce the perversion of invoking love, loyalty or submission to force somebody to pay the price for my sin. I reject and renounce the deception of living in supposed love, loyalty and submission to pay the price for somebody else's sin. I reject and renounce the spirit of entitlement. True sowing is necessary, and there is a proper crop that comes from every seed that is sown.

I reject and renounce embracing visions that require exploitation of the people of God, and legitimizing those visions in the name of God. I reject and renounce my sin of using popularity to normalize iniquity, especially moral impurity, and to lower your holy standards. I reject and renounce the sin of staying in an abusive situation to the point that I have not possessed my birthright. It was sin for Israel to be comfortable in the mountains and not exterminate the Canaanites. It is sin to stay in a place that I am not supposed to be for the sake of peace, if it keeps me from possessing my birthright. Bring this cleansing forward through every generation and every branch of my family line. Cleanse me from this iniquity and from the Canaanite curse.

I receive this cleansing. In the name of Jesus of Nazareth, I command every demonic structure and entity that was empowered by those sins and iniquities to leave now and never return. I extend this cleansing and this freedom to my spouse and to my physical and spiritual seed to a thousand generations. Father, give me your strategy, your timing and your methods to finish exterminating the Canaanite enemies from my life. Teach me how to disengage from entanglements, and to move into a place where I have the time and permission to nurture the gifts that you have given me. Teach me and supernaturally aid me. You not only give strategy, but you do miracles. I claim the same measure of victory that Israel had when every Canaanite soldier was killed, including the general. Exterminate every vestige of the Canaanite curse from me, my family line and future generations. I ask this in the name of Jesus Christ of Nazareth. Amen.

Blessing Prayer For Exhorter

God has blessed you with the gift of being a change-agent in your world. You are inspirational and a great motivator who can inspire others to do exploits for God. God designed you to long to put Him and His glory on a large stage.

You are fun to be around. You are outgoing, intensely people-oriented and relational. I bless your ability to cross every kind of barrier, socially, racially, economically and religiously. You can relate to everybody wherever they are and strike up a conversation about heart matters, because you are adaptable and accepted by everybody. I bless your ability to never meet a stranger. You find the key to their heart in a short time. You can relate to the God-shaped vacuum in people. God opens it up to you. I bless you with meeting people where they are and taking them to the next step that God has for them.

I bless your gift for communication. I bless your words, the urgency and frequency with which you speak. God made you to be verbally expressive, and it is good. I bless you to speak of spirit things, life-giving things. You are called to know God and to make Him known. I bless you with magnifying the greatness of God. Ask God to give you His voice that is not hindered by the legitimacy needs of the soul. When you have touched God and are sharing Him, other people open up their spirits to your spirit to receive revelation about Him. I bless you with maturity and growth, being conformed to Jesus that will keep your gift totally spirit-to-spirit.

You are designed to be relational. I bless your ability to light up a room with your presence. You are energized by being with people. You value face-to-face time. You are inclusive. I bless you for bringing others into your circle of influence without compromising your view of God. I bless you for loving God, loving people and wanting to bring the two together. Your relationships are the vehicle for bringing together people with the reality of God. I bless your skill in creating and sustaining relationships. It is one of your most obvious and easiest strengths, but your deepest strength is how quickly you see truth in the Word of God. You can reveal the nature of God and new facets of God to people who already know a lot about Him.

You easily transition from small talk, to relationship, to evangelism. You can speak of faith to a pre-Christian so that he receives it in his spirit when his soul is not interested. You can receive people where they are but challenge them practically, simply and powerfully to see God bigger. You bring great pleasure to Jesus' heart as you incarnate this portion of himself.

As Jesus listened to his Father, He led His disciples by relationship, persuasion, time and attention. You are at your finest when you are listening to your Father, like Jesus, as you reach, teach and lead by influence, persuasion and consensus. You can smoothly bring a group of people to a course of action they need to take. You have a coaching style of leadership.

You are a master of reconciliation over disunity and independent spirits because you can celebrate differences. You are tactful, diplomatic and approachable. You can smoothly bring a word in an acceptable way. You are an ambassador, a minister, a friend, confidant, listener, affirmer and counselor. The rest of the body needs your skillset.

You are a visionary. You tend to see a broader picture, the largest number of people. You can lay a vision for a diverse group. You are sensitive to the timing and movement of God. You are flexible and quick to see opportunities, and change a plan to take advantage of what God is doing at the moment. You are not intimidated by new ideas, new opportunities, new potential, new challenges or new truth.

Your greatest calling is to know God and to reveal Him to others. You are gifted to see God in Scripture. You get so much out of the Word of God with little time and effort. That is an extraordinary gifting from God—to extract nuggets of truths from the Word. I bless you to go vertical with God, hear from Him and discipline yourself to see Him in ways others do not, so that you can point out truths others overlook. Jesus revealed His Father in parables, in lessons from life, and you are marvelous at presenting a story. Your teaching style is narrative and illustrative. You speak the message of parable to meet people where they are.

People-pleasing is a battle for everybody at times; depending on our wounding and where we get our significance and legitimacy. I bless you to win the battle of people-pleasing in order to know God and possess your birthright. God forced world-changers Moses and Paul to get to know Him in a desert season alone, so they could become mighty in spirit in what He called them to do. In prison God gave Paul revelation that people have benefited from for 2000 years, as he authored the majority of the epistles, the theology, the teaching and practices of the early church. We are the recipients 2000 years later through his exhorter gift. I bless you with getting God's picture of your God-given abilities of persuasion and leadership and His desire to take you to something that you don't even dream for yourself right now.

I bless you with living by principle and risking reaction, offense, alienation or rejection for the truth of God without compromise or soft choices. I bless you with the strength of character, wisdom and grace to confront what needs to be confronted. Paul the exhorter said, "If I were a slave of men, I would not be a slave of God." I bless you with freedom from the need to be liked when God leads you to confront. You will be living in God's highest authority and life-giving anointing when you confront as Jesus did with grace and love. I bless you with placing relationship in its proper place on the altar before God and desiring holiness and obedience to Him. The pleasure of the Father is on you when you take the attitude of Jesus toward sin; that it must be dealt with and that He paid the ultimate price to deal with it.

Love and faith and service are markers of the exhorter. You are very busy, function on little sleep, wear many hats and are involved in many projects. You do an abundance of things and take advantage of many opportunities. That is how God made you. Model your life on how Jesus lived his life. He said, "I have finished all that you have given me to do." Do the work that your Father gives you to do, and don't default into getting your significance from being busy. I bless you to know that your plans are God's plan. Find out where He is at work and join Him. Great synergy and great blessing are released, beyond your natural abilities, when you cooperate with God. Often the good is the greatest hindrance to the best. Don't settle for an Ishmael, when God wants to give you an Isaac. I bless you to discover the one thing God wants you to do.

I bless you with taking your God-designed dominion over time and timing. I bless you with not being defeated by time, but having responsibility in time issues. That's who God made you to be. I bless your supernatural design for bringing God's timing and seasons into reality. God designed you to know and to mark the seasons of God because you know the mind of God and you are sensitive to his appropriate timing.

I bless you to know the principle of sowing and reaping. I bless you as you righteously respond to pain and see redemptive lessons in personal pain and suffering. "No pain, no gain." Paul the exhorter wrote one of the most sublime passages in the Bible in Philippians 3:8-10. That is vintage exhorter. You earn authority that comes through embracing personal pain and suffering, so that God releases your authority in His kingdom.

Go to God and get His perspective on the largeness of your calling. I bless you to use the strengths of your skillset: confidence, strength, boldness and commanding presence in all areas of your God-given authority. I bless you with time, ability, resources and pathway to develop areas of your greatest potential. I bless your call to reveal God in His greatness, His holiness, and His perfection. I bless you to be who God made you to be as a reflection of Christ. Continue to be your joyous, extravagant self. Press hard, run fast, pursue the limitless horizon. I bless you to unleash the Spirit and the Word in the context of community to the glory of God. I bless you to be a reflection of the nature of Christ wherever you go. I bless you in Jesus' name. Amen.

5. Giver

Prayer Of Renunciation Of The Midianite Curse

Almighty God and heavenly Father, you are the God of time. Time is the first thing you created on the first day. Therefore, it is the first fruits of your creation. The first-fruit of everything is dedicated to you, and thereby it is made holy. Since I am a child of God, your intent is that I live in holy time. You do not intend for the seasons of my life to be devoured. I acknowledge that the defilement and the devouring is my fault. Open the books on my family lines and reveal the roots of this curse. I reject and renounce the spirit of control in every branch of my family lines. I repudiate the faithlessness that kept some of my forefathers from possessing their birthright.

I reject the god of comfort and security, and I say that you are able to give tremendous comfort to your people when they possess their birthright. I confess, reject and renounce the deception from the enemy that it is right for me to postpone possessing my birthright until a more convenient time.

I reject and renounce running ahead of your time and behind your time. Cleanse my generational lines of these iniquities. Remove the Midianite curse from my life, my family and my physical and spiritual seed. Nail the curse to the cross of Jesus Christ, and render it null and void.

Father, I proclaim my dependence on you. I want to live by faith, to depend on you, and to possess my birthright. The spirit is willing, but the flesh is weak. I have a lifestyle of fear and a history of seeking comfort and security. Just as you did the miracle for Gideon, and as you sustained him when nobody would sustain him, sustain me when I have to pursue my birthright and nobody understands and sustains me. Save me not only from the enemy but also from myself.

At every place where the enemy used to curse and where you desire to release blessings, let your will be done. Release the blessings that you have decreed for me in the seasons that you decree. I pray for Israel, with the giver gift, that you would protect them from the evil one and that you would bring them to true spiritual liberty from all curses. Have mercy on giver cities and nations and release the riches there, so that the people of God in this season can be restored to the fullness of their birthright. Thank you in advance for sanctifying time for me and for my generations. In Jesus' name I pray. Amen.

Blessing Prayer For Giver

Giver, God chose you in Christ before the creation of the world to be who you are and to be gifted just as you are. You are not as out front as some of the other gifts, but they need you. I bless you to be enriched and enlarged in God's design of you and to come into alignment with His plans for you. God loves your gift, and He celebrates the complexity of your life. I bless you for your diversity. You have done many things, and yet you would like to do, know how to do and can do many more things. You are involved in many projects, interests and activities. You are adaptable and flexible. You do not fit easily into stereotypes or molds.

I bless your nurturing, celebrating family and your desire to have family comfortable in relationship. Nurture is a big component of your gift. It is an expression of the nature of God. I bless you as you release into your family line everything that God has in the gold mine of your inheritance. You have the God-given calling to weave people together into a relational culture; into a dynamic that is greater than the sum of its parts. I bless you with representing the heart of the Father who is a God of community. You represent his desire to create, nurture and sustain community because you are made in His image. God delights in your desire to be life-giving to the family, to the community of faith and to the world around you.

I bless your desire, ability and authority to birth, nurture and protect new ideas and new things. The prophet gift needs you for the synergy released when you and the prophet team together in the alignment and timing that God has designed for the two of you. Receive the way that God made you to contribute to His life in the body of Christ.

I bless your generational worldview. You are focused on preparing the way for others after you. God designed you to release generational blessings. God calls you to bless and to raise blessing to a high level. You fulfill your birthright when you invoke life-giving generational blessings for your family and community and produce life-giving systems that express God's design.

I bless your alertness and creativity to see options, opportunities and possibilities that others miss. You are opportunistic in seizing the moment. I bless your success in less than ideal circumstances where all the resources are not available. I bless you to maximize imperfect environments or skill sets and create something new and lasting; finding the "win-win" proposition for yourself and others at the same time.

I bless your heart's desire to see people saved and the kingdom of God expanded as an eternal generational inheritance. The synergy of the kingdom is complete as you help other gifts bring unbelievers into the kingdom by providing the resources and identifying fruit that is ripe for picking.

I bless you for your independence and how you stand alone. It is a positive trait when it partners with acknowledging your need for God. Independence can be very powerful when it is totally surrendered to God and in partnership with Him. Pride in personal competence is a challenging occupational hazard of the giver gift. I bless you with the ability to overcome the temptation of considering yourself to be self-contained, having the authority, the money, the influence, the resources and/or the security to do whatever you feel led to do. I bless you to be vigilant and not to let this strength be corrupted into control, which is a perversion of your gift.

I bless your strong desire to maintain your own uniqueness, but I bless you with understanding the interdependence of the gifts personally and in the community of faith. Focus on what you have to add to the other gifts with the cooperation, partnership, alignment and synergy that God intends. Trust God to work in them to accomplish a "win-win" proposition with all the gifts.

I bless you with understanding and an awareness of where your gift gets tripped up. I bless you with healing of the wounds that have caused your basic trust to be fractured, and caused you to respond out of woundedness. I bless you to grow into your greatest potential living in the authority and honor of the giver gift.

I bless you to win the battle of gratitude. God commanded the giver nation of Israel to remember and to celebrate His presence, His works and His wonders. I bless you with the desire to celebrate God's past intervention. I bless you with the foundation of worship, a lifestyle of looking for and seeing God's fingerprints on every part of life. I bless your leading others to recognize the work of God, and calling attention to Him as He provides big things and little things.

I bless you as a networker, bringing people together, persuading and inspiring people to do things that they would not normally do. Nobody networks like the giver, and you delight in introducing people and building through relationship. Develop your gift of being intentionally life-giving from your spirit to the spirit of others.

Giver, you are pragmatic and a practical peacemaker. You are not confrontational by nature. You are diplomatic; not wanting to offend. In dealing with people, you get disproportionate return on your effort. You can work with people who have conflicting views and theologies for the sake of a group or a project. You relate to a wide range of very different people. It is as if you are the hub of a wheel, and the spokes radiate out from you. Without the hub, the wheel could not move forward to accomplish a God-given objective. I bless your ability in the community of believers to keep the other gifts related and properly focused.

You are careful of your reputation and that of others. You speak of what is good, righteous and commendable in other people. I bless your caring about the reputation of the kingdom and of the bride of Christ.

You resist manipulation of information. You don't like to have anything withheld from you. You have an intuitive sense for what is false. I bless your gift of discernment in this area.

You usually do the right things, and your acquaintances would say of you that you are a nice person. I bless you to go deeper with God and deepen your spiritual motivation of holiness, which is pleasing to Him.

You find favor in money and resources flowing to you without human explanation or reason. You find bargains, and people give you discounts. At times you may find yourself fighting the temptation to use money as a point of security or as a means of gratification, entitlement, reward or control. I bless your spirit with the ability to overcome these temptations.

I bless you to give well and wisely where there is the greatest potential for eternal return on your investment. When your giving is exercised with God's wisdom, it makes others grateful for God's generosity and He gets the credit and the glory. I bless you with learning how to give in ways that nurture the spirit to form a deeper and richer community.

You tend not to see patterns from the past. You also tend to rationalize and often to blame. You resent it when someone confronts you over issues that are more than a week old. I bless you with the ability to learn from life experiences and see things from God's perspective. I bless you with the ability to react with grace when others point out patterns that you do not see.

I bless you with being secure because of your relationship with God. I bless you with letting God take your faith to new levels. Sometimes faith is hard for you, because you want to avoid risk, and it may lead to fear and control. I bless you with winning the battle against control. It's not God's design for you to play it safe and only do the things that you are sure that you can handle. I bless you with faith that is greater than fear of risk.

Stewardship is the essence of living by faith. You receive resources from God to do what He calls you to do. God's standard for the giver is stewardship of all, because everything belongs to Him. The principle of stewardship relates to life, potential, gifts, resources and relationships. It extends to long-term life-giving generational changes. You are meant to establish relationship and invest in generational blessings that you will pass on. I bless you with being the model of a steward of everything God gives.

I bless you with being settled in who you are in Christ, your identity in Him and your legitimacy as a covenant child of the King of kings, as you partner with Him in intimate relationship.

You are meant to interface powerfully with the other gifts. The community of the gifts needs you to possess your birthright in your unique way. That is the dignity, honor and beauty of the God-seeking giver. You are God's choice for some significant things. I bless you with moving into your full birthright. I bless you in Jesus' name. Amen.

6. Ruler

Prayer Of Renunciation Of Jotham's Curse

Almighty God and heavenly Father, you are the God of covenant, of community, of institutions and of government. You have designed human institutions to be life-giving, to be generational and to be strategic. Institutions that deliver death instead of life are the work of the enemy and not the work of your hands. Open the books in my generational lines and show me the roots of this curse. I confess, reject and renounce the sins of ingratitude to those who have been life-givers to me. I confess the sin of covenant-breaking regarding life-giving relationships. I confess, reject and renounce the sins of sedition and lawlessness. I repudiate the lie that legitimacy can come from having power through an institution.

Father, you have designed some institutions to have great power. You use institutions to transform societies, but I reject the deception that legitimacy comes through institutional power. I have seen the curse of Jotham operating in my life and in my culture. The death that it brings is painful, and yet you are a just God, and you only empower Jotham's curse where there has been covenant-breaking. So I accept the justice of your judgment.

Father, I embrace the justice of your restoration. Because of the blood of the Lamb and the word of my confession, those iniquities are now under the blood and the enemy is disempowered. In the name of Jesus Christ of Nazareth, I command every demonic entity that has been operating through Jotham's curse to leave me, my family line, my ministry, my business and my physical and spiritual seed to a thousand generations. Teach me about covenant, and empower me to be a covenant-keeper. Release the blessing of freedom of movement in my life so that I walk on a smooth road.

I bless the institutions that you have chosen for me. Give me your grace to stay in covenant with those who are covenant-breakers. Give me the grace to finish the course that you have laid out for me. Release the blessings that have been blocked that are rightfully mine. Release them into my life, my family, my ministry, my business and my institutions. I ask this in the name of Jesus Christ, because He kept covenant and finished His course. Amen.

Blessing Prayer For Ruler

I bless your leadership call to organize and administer social units, groups of people and resources. Your maximum leadership quotient is based on God's gifting, being submitted to God's law and being life-giving to those around you. I bless you as an implementer who takes a vision and effectively implements a plan from incremental steps. You know the resources available and needed to reach a goal. You can visualize the final result of a major undertaking by a group, and at the same time break down major goals into smaller achievable tasks for individuals, as Nehemiah did. I bless how you pull together a group based on loyalty to own a problem together. You need loyalty and confidence from those who are being directed and served.

I bless your strength of seeing the opportunity to use imperfect, broken people and position them to draw the best out of them without letting their brokenness damage the whole. I bless how you position others for success while minimizing their weaknesses that would hinder a project. You can overlook character faults, woundedness, inexperience, and immaturity in people who otherwise have valuable skills to offer in reaching the goal. I bless you for bringing out of people the very best that they can contribute to the whole group.

I bless your ability to know what you should and should not delegate to others. You can orchestrate the details by delegating, and you do not involve yourself in details in order to focus on the ultimate goal.

I bless your ability to thrive under pressure and also to motivate people to do more than they think they can do. I bless how you challenge people to go beyond anything they have done before, but you are sensitive to know when you are putting other people under too much pressure. Jesus has given you the life-giving treasure of himself in you with which to be life-giving; even when you are expecting people to go beyond where they have ever been.

God has given you the gift of being task-oriented, focused on the objective. I bless your ability to endure reaction from insiders and outsiders to reach a higher envisioned goal, as you appropriately balance suggestions, appeals and valid complaints of those on the team. I bless you to be totally in tune with God and doing what He says to do. You do not need the affirmation of other people when you've heard from God. You can receive your vindication from God and wait a long time for it. Your example is Jesus, who was willing to be humbled and accepted the reviling of others to bring freedom to the world. He endured the scorn, despising the shame (Hebrews 12:2), when sinful men tortured Him and crucified Him, thus bringing salvation to us.

Some will not appreciate the work that you are doing or the way you are doing it. Some will resist and resent you, and others will be jealous of you. I bless you to carry on, because God has designed you to be less influenced by public opinion than most. You can endure opposition and criticism by those over, under and around you. I bless you to press on when people who should support you don't.

I bless you as you inspire and encourage a team through cheerfulness, approval, praise, challenge, personal sensitivity and nurture. I bless you to give explanation to each strategic part of individual roles in the big picture. Everybody needs to know that their role is vital, even indispensable, and where their contribution fits into the overall scheme. I bless you to not overlook individual needs of workers and not to view them as resources, as pieces on a chessboard to accomplish goals or tasks. I bless you to shepherd people. It is a beautiful part of being a ruler when you see your call to shepherd the people who are involved in the organization or objective at hand.

I bless your independence in a positive way. You have no welfare mentality. You don't look to others for solutions. You are not into blame, either yourself or others. I bless your strength of figuring out how to fix it when something goes wrong. You are willing to own problems and accomplish the task rather than wasting time blaming and assigning fault.

I bless you with a singleness of heart and the ability to focus on what God has called you to do. The result of your Godly work is disproportionate to the investment of resources. The example of Nehemiah is your heritage as a ruler. You get results that are beyond brilliant administrative skills when you are partnering with God, doing the main thing or the one thing He has called you to do.

I bless how you see the open door God places before you, and use inadequate resources to accomplish extraordinary things. This is how God made you, and it brings him pleasure when you accomplish that. When you are following God, at the right place, at the right time, doing the right thing, God's grace is upon you to find resources that others don't see and weave them together for a hugely disproportionate impact. Your Father is pleased when you do the impossible, so that He gets the glory when the only explanation for it is "God was in it." He is tapping deep into what He placed within you, and your Father delights in watching you in operation. That is His great joy.

I bless you to pursue the full range of dominion that God intended for you. You are so gifted and talented in the natural, that it would take two lifetimes to do everything you are good at. You look at anything and want to make it bigger and better. Beware of the danger of success, when you are talented and gifted enough to succeed on your merits. Your success can become a trap as you camp out on success; when God wants you to partner in the spiritual realm and do the supernatural, and accomplish what only God can do.

I bless your diversity. You have your finger in many pies, and you do it with great skill and grace. You seem to be good at everything you touch. You organize and you lead. You see opportunities and possibilities. There are things you may do that will bring you pleasure and leave a legacy in your community. Nevertheless, the good is the eternal enemy of the best. Sometimes you can settle for man's plans and fall short of God's design. Jesus is your model, as He finished the one thing his Father sent Him to do (John 17:4). On the cross Jesus said, "It is finished." He got the key thing done. There is no greater satisfaction at the end of the day or of a lifetime, than to know that you have glorified your Father by doing exactly what He wanted you to do. I bless you to find your greatest fulfillment there, as His kingdom will be extended and the world will be changed for generations to come.

A potential weakness of your gift is compromise, settling for what is OK instead of God's best. That is not God's highest and best for you. God designed you for living in righteousness, holiness and life-giving. On these values you stand or fall. I bless you to use the moral authority that comes from submitting to God as the basis of your authority. Where you have integrity, you will have spiritual authority, greater influence and everything necessary to lead people. As you do that, your moral and spiritual authority will grow and you will give life to your community as the righteous leader God wants you to be.

I bless your joy and fulfillment in seeing all the parts come together in a finished product. Hebrews 12 says that for the joy set before Him, Jesus endured the cross where He paid in full the total legal penalty for sin. Because of that finished work on the cross, we have freedom. I bless you to live in freedom and fight for freedom for others. I bless you in the principle of freedom that is the fruit of effectively weaving together resources, principles and blessings to move toward your birthright. I bless you in the fullness of your calling to show the world what freedom can be.

I bless your God-given authority in a high level of generational anointing. You desire to impart generational blessings. God's call is for you to concern yourself with the spirit realm in your family, purging and cleansing the generational lines and building a generational blessing and heritage for the generations after you. Your birthright is to invest in a community of faith, to cleanse others from the defilement coming down from their ancestors, and to build a deposit of blessing that will carry them for generations after you leave. I bless you as you step into the greatness that God has called you to and become passionate about cleansing your spiritual line and building a spiritual heritage for your physical and spiritual seed. You were made to leave a great spiritual heritage as you accrue a high level of spiritual dominion over spiritual issues and pass on to your physical and spiritual offspring generational blessings that will pursue them all their days.

I bless you with expanding your thinking about your gift. It is more than dominion over people as a leader of organizations. That is a portion of your birthright, but that is not the original mandate of God. Based on the sixth day of creation, God designed you for dominion over the animal kingdom, although you have not lived it yet. Your birthright is to set the spiritual dynamic of the day, and to call the right living creatures to do the right thing whether in motion, sound, color, etc. You may be nowhere near there yet, but I bless you with releasing what God has placed in you that has been carried for hundreds of generations since Adam and Eve without seeing its full expression. I bless you in your generation with unleashing the power that God has placed in creation. I bless you with living in the original blessing that God gave to you, son of Adam and son of the Second Adam.

As a ruler you may not have developed in your capacity for gathering and leading the human spirit. On the sixth day of creation God created the human spirit and placed it in the first man. The spirit is the righteous domain of the ruler not just command, power and control.

I bless you as you grow and become accomplished in your spiritual DNA of leading the spirits of others. I bless your capacity for fathering the human spirit, for knowing when to build and when to war, that comes with your gift. You are called to know more about how to guide, lead, shape and use the spirit, as well as the soul. I bless your call to father by nurturing the human spirit, not just the soul. I bless you in your challenge to understand the spirit as profoundly as you understand the soul. I bless you as you nurture your spirit and rely on the power of heaven to supplement what you can do in the natural. Mobilize the spirits of people-- leading, grouping, deploying their spirits. Create the synergy of one person's spirit with another, of one team's spirit with another team's spirit.

You were made to father the spirit, not just the soul. I bless you as you understand how to bless the human spirit for the good of the kingdom of God. I bless you as you live in your anointing to nurture the human spirit, and weave together a human community based on oneness of spirit, not common goals for the soul. When the spirit is dominant, it draws out the best of the soul. The soul operates at a better level when it is under the leadership of the spirit. I bless you to use the resources of the spirit and the resources of heaven in fathering the next generation. Amen.

7. Mercy

Prayer Of Renunciation Of The Ammonite Curse

Almighty God and heavenly Father, I rejoice in calling you Father. I come to you acknowledging that you are the Righteous Judge of the universe and my loving Father. I have been deceived, and I have acted wrongly out of my deception. I reject the lie that I need to, or that I could earn your favor or your love. I reject and renounce my focus on human favor. I reject and renounce every incident in my family line where somebody chose to embrace human perspectives instead of your perspective. I reject every human stigma that is contrary to your view of me. I reject and renounce the cultural pressure that causes me to not excel, lest I make others look bad. I reject and renounce the cowardice of failing to speak up about things that are evil, lest I offend those around me. I reject and renounce the iniquity of valuing the favor of men more than possessing my birthright. Forgive me for those iniquities.

Cover those things with the blood of Jesus in every branch of my family line. Bring that cleansing from the beginning of time to the present, to my physical and spiritual seed to a thousand generations. I command every devouring spirit that has been empowered by these curses to leave now in the name of Jesus, and to go and never return to me, my spiritual seed or my physical descendants.

The issue for me is to learn to love you, not for me to purchase your love. Anoint my eyes with the ointment of Revelation 3:18, so I can see your love in the daily events of my life. In every act of service to you, reveal more of your love for me. As I see your love, cause my love for you to well up within me. Create a fire within me to possess my birthright. I see in part, and I know in part. There is so much you want to show me that I am not able to receive.

Father, enlarge my spirit and my capacity to receive the passion of heaven, and fill that space with the passion that Jesus had. Release the blessings that come when the Ammonite curse is broken. Those blessings are compensation for the pains in my life that came from your hand. Do a supernatural work in me, and in my world, to position me to possess my birthright.

There is nothing too hard for you. There is no area of brokenness that you cannot redeem. I wait in expectation for you to work in me, through me and around me, so that I can possess my birthright and so that the rivers of living water will flow from me to the world around me. Sever every tie to every unclean thing in the present or the past that would hold me back from experiencing your best. Fill every place that the enemy has vacated. Seal the work that has been done in me. Enforce every righteous decree. You are my King, and I have your protection because you love me, not because I deserve it. I proclaim your love, I celebrate your love and I desire to live in your love. I ask these things in the mighty name of Jesus Christ. Amen.

Blessing Prayer For Mercy

I bless you and honor you for your special place as the most complex and most sensitive of the gifts. You are the crown jewel of God's creation. The apostle John is the model for your gift, with his intimate and confidential relationship with Jesus.

I bless you for your safety for those who are wounded. You tend to attract people who are having mental and emotional distress. I bless your initiative toward wounded ones. You know who is feeling rejected, excluded or wounded. People, even strangers, can safely share their pain. You can touch a grieving heart with your quick release of tears.

I bless your deep power of compassion, the most healing of all human emotions. A biblical model for what mercy does is the Good Samaritan, who was sensitive and responsive to the needs of the wounded man when other travelers passed by on the other side. He identified with the man who fell among thieves. He had courage to translate caring into practical action. He did what he did because he was the man that he was.

I bless your loyalty to those you love. You are quick to take up the offenses of family and friends when they are rejected or mistreated. You draw away from those who are insensitive to others.

I bless your ability to sense genuine love. You have a large number of acquaintances and people who enjoy you, but you may have only a few close intimate friends. I bless your need for deep friendships in which there is mutual commitment and closeness. You have great expectations from friendships and can be deeply hurt by disappointments in friends. Jesus is your only Friend who will never disappoint.

I bless the totally different language that you speak, the language of the heart that is sometimes too deep for logic or for words. I bless you as you try to speak the language that your spirit does not have vocabulary for. I bless how you can recognize and capture God's presence in the ordinary events of everyday life. You see the beauty in the smallest things. You take time to smell the roses and appreciate unplanned moments of goodness. You communicate so much with your eyes, your touch and your attention. You are frustrated when others don't understand this. You don't like people to try to re-engineer you into being something you are not.

I bless your desire for closeness. You measure acceptance by physical closeness and quality time together. You crave intimacy of soul, physical touch, hugs, communication and contact. God designed you for intimacy in body, soul and spirit. He will make a way for its holy and righteous expression by his grace.

I bless you with God's perspective on pain. Without his perspective, you can see no spiritual benefit to pain and suffering. When you avoid pain, the discipline of God may be wasted, because he builds righteousness and maturity through the discipline of pain. You may react to God's purposes in allowing people to suffer, and you want to remove the cause of pain quickly. I bless you to keep your eye on the joy set before you: to share in his holiness, a harvest of righteousness and peace for those who are trained by discipline, by pain, by struggle.

I bless you to turn to God for comfort when you are hurting. You can be sensitive; easily injured by the words and actions of others. You have a hard time healing from injury and processing and expressing what you are feeling. Others say to you, "Just get over it." This lack of understanding can cause you to withdraw and shut down. I bless you to pursue the God of all comfort and the Father of mercies; who will move into the pain and minister life where healing is needed.

I bless you with healthy, God-ordained boundaries. You can become a burden-bearer for burdens God does not intend you to bear, if you absorb pain from people who want to dump their pain on you. You don't have to absorb everybody's burdens. Jesus daily bears your burdens. His yoke is easy, and His burden is light (Matthew 11:29-30). Trust Him to help you process emotions. I bless you to breathe deeper, live more freely and connect more with people and God as you refuse to carry unholy burdens.

I bless your decision-making processes. You tend to be slow to make transitions based on emotional processing. It's not wrong; it's uniquely you. You do not like change; you require longer to disengage emotionally and re-engage in the next thing. I bless you as you let God take you through this process in his time.

I bless your ability to experience life differently. God wired you to operate intuitively. You feel the heart of God and make significant decisions based on your heart. That is your God-given appropriate language. I bless you for connecting with your heart, and putting the other gifts in touch with processing that is spirit to spirit. You hear from God but have difficulty explaining the "why". The first six gifts typically hear God with their mind in a linear, logical way, but you hear and understand God with your spirit before your mind can explain what your spirit heard. I bless you to be free to say, "I don't know how I know. I just know. I don't have words."

I bless you to represent God in tough love. You hate to confront anybody. You may find it hard to be firm and decisive because you don't want to offend. You tend to avoid decisions and firmness until not deciding will cause greater hurt. When you are operating below the maximum of your gifting, you may bless what is broken or even sinful. An enabler will sympathize with those who violate God's standards to preserve the feelings of others. I bless your design by God to be absorbed in his holiness so that there is no way to enable brokenness or sinfulness.

You do not like to take sides or choose between two people. You may be seen as indecisive, because you do not want to hurt anybody or say they are wrong. Your highest authority will come when you are so aligned with God's perspective that you can appeal to those in sin and encourage them to come into alignment with God. Your model is Jesus who only did what He saw his Father doing. I bless you as you embrace your responsibility to see that which is clean and complete and aligned with God and bless others to raise the standard.

I bless you to let Father God re-father you and show you who you really are. Let Him heal your wounds of earthly fathering and authorities. I bless you to let your heavenly Father establish you in your spirit. I bless you to be deeply fathered by Him, until there is no fear, insecurity, roots of rejection or abandonment, so that you have freedom, wholeness, willingness to risk, inclusion and belongingness. I bless you to step into your proper place in your heavenly Father, so you can live out your birthright.

Your spirit is not meant to be passive or to allow injustice. I bless you to win the battle against the victim mindset that attracts infirmity, financial devouring, physical abuse, sexual assault or dishonor. You are a covenant child of the Most High God. You have dignity, honor, authority and a special place in God's dominion. I bless you to rise up and live in all that you are in God.

You dislike and avoid warfare until you are pushed into a corner. When you see the pain others suffer, you can be drawn into spiritual warfare as a last resort. You are intended to master the art of worship as warfare. I bless you as you lift up the glory of God, His power, His miracles, His works, and His names, reminding all of heaven, earth and hell that we serve God Most High. That is a radical disruption of the powers of evil around you.

I bless your creativity that raises the water table of the spiritual life of your faith community. You are drawn to the arts that allow you to express your love of God, or vent the pain you feel or say visually what you do not have words for. Your sensitive spirit can express prayer, praise, reflection, peace, forgiveness or reconciliation and connect them with the five senses. You appreciate creative expression and beauty in the spiritual life of the church.

Your spirit knows you are made to worship. You seek the face of God in intimacy. You are called to fulfillment by connecting with the Spirit of God, and easily going into his presence to absorb his holiness and glory and bring others there. You can release the holiness of the glory of God into the world, and I bless you as you impart the blessing of presence and alignment to people, land, the environment and buildings. I bless you to absorb the holiness of God in the Holy of Holies, and then release the blessing of His holiness and to align that which is crooked or warped.

On the seventh day God aligned, sanctified and celebrated everything He had already made. You celebrate the rightness of everything God has done and is doing. You know what right alignment is when all the pieces are in their right place. You are alert to how the parts relate to the whole. You are right to feel in your spirit that there is something more. I bless your innate knowing that there is another dimension of beauty, excellence and perfection where everything is so right it resonates in heavenly keys and rhythms. I bless you with moving toward alignment in the spirit realm where the spirit brings out the best of the soul, and the spirit and the soul are releasing the finest of what the body can do. That is your birthright.

I bless you with becoming the guardian of God's alignment with your blessing of presence. I bless you as God releases you into the fullness of who you were made to be -- knowing your Father, blessing others and releasing holiness to their spirits. You are called to be large-spirited. I bless you with authority and dominion in the community of the spirit. I bless you in the name of the 7-fold Spirit of the true and living God. Amen.

Helpful Charts

The following charts come from Charles Wale's book, *Designed for Fulfillment*, and are helpful for comparing and contrasting the redemptive gifts discussed in chapter 1.[111]

Seven In Scripture

Gifts	Days Of Creation	Furniture In The Tabernacle	Compound Names Of God	Churches In Revelation	Last Sayings Of Christ On The Cross
Prophet	Light	Brazen altar	Jehovah-Jireh God Provides	Ephesus	Father, forgive them, for they do not know what they are doing
Servant	Atmosphere	Bronze laver	Jehovah-Rophe God heals	Smyrna	I tell you the truth, today you will be with me in paradise
Teacher	Dry Land	Table of showbread	Jehovah-Nissi God is my banner	Pergamum	Dear woman, here is your son; here is your mother.
Exhorter	Sun, moon, and stars	Golden lamp stand	Jehovah-Shalom God is my peace	Thyatira	My God, my God why have you forsaken me?
Giver	Life in sea and air	Altar of incense	Jehovah-Rohi God is my shepherd	Sardis	I am thirsty
Ruler	Land animals and humans	Ark of the covenant	Jehovah-Tsidkenu God is my righteousness	Philadelphia	It is finished
Mercy	Rest	Mercy seat	Jehovah-Shammah God is there	Laodicea	Father, into your hands I commit my spirit

---

[111] Note the following:
- "Seven in Scripture" comes from page 137 of his book.
- "Redemptive Gifts Grid I" is found on page 135.
- "Redemptive Gifts Grid II" is located on page 136.

Redemptive Gifts Grid I

Gift	Principle vs. Battlefield	Authority	Birthright	Major Weaknesses
Prophet	**Design** vs. Fractured relationships	Principles for speaking life, light, and truth that call forth destiny	To help others live in their destiny by providing vision on God's design	Non-relational Judgmental Bitterness and unforgivenes
Servant	**Authority** vs. Mindset of victimization	Pray for leaders, restore families, love the hard cases	To be a life-giver to others, especially leaders. To provide the cleansing and authority others require for their destiny	Battle for self-worth Worry/anxiety Enabling
Teacher	**Responsibility** vs. Selective responsibility	Generational blessing as they bring forth fruit	To know God's deep truths and to know him experientially. To reveal the presence of God to others	Passive Selective responsibility Sight vs faith Doctrine vs. intimacy
Exhorter	**Sowing And Reaping** vs. Denial	Influence through relationships. Reconciliation to God and others	To reveal God to others. To mobilize large numbers of people to act on God's will	People-pleasing Poor time management Compromise
Giver	**Stewardship** vs. Ownership and independence	To detect, bring forth, protect, and nurture new birth	To release life-giving generational blessings into the family line. To produce life-giving systems through holiness and intimacy with God	Independence Hypocrisy Manipulation and control
Ruler	**Freedom** vs. Exploitation	Highest level of generational blessings that bring freedom	To release spiritual generational blessings physically and spiritually by honoring God's agenda	Insensitivity Ethics/integrity Substituting his agenda for God's agenda
Mercy	**Fulfillment** vs. Futility	Intimacy with God and alignment	To release the holiness of God into their environment. To come into the presence of God and worship God in all of life	Impurity Mixture of holy and unholy Enabling to protect from pain

Redemptive Gifts Grid II

Gift	Foundational Principles	Demonic Strongholds	Root Iniquity	Essential Virtues	Curses On The Birthright	Causes Of The Curse	Blessings Needed For Effectiveness
Prophet	Purpose, design, and truth	Fractured relationships	The rights of Individuals	Being a rebuilder	**Aramean** Can't get justice	Adultery or molestation in the family line	**Hosea** Favor
Servant	Authority	Victim Spirit	Peace at any cost	Walking in dominion	**Moabite** No platform for success	Poverty spirit, fear of loss, inability to grasp identity	**Esther** Secure borders, resources for life
Teacher	Responsibility	Religious spirit	Selective responsibility	Sanctifying his family	**Philistine** Lacks key resources, one piece missing blocks project	Using religiosity to legitimize wrong behavior	**Daniel** Supernatural strategies, receiving from God
Exhorter	Sowing and reaping	The cult of comfort	Denial	Embracing the pain	**Canaanite** Oppressive work load	Denial and entitlement. Using influence to persuade others to do wrong	**Moses** Time to develop finest abilities
Giver	Stewardship	Ownership	Control	Walking by faith	**Midianite** Seasonal devouring of money & family relationships	Putting personal comfort ahead of responsibility to nurture family	**Job** Accruing capital
Ruler	Freedom	Predator Spirit	Exploitation	Being life-giving	**Jotham's** Betrayal from within	Covenant-breaking. Lawlessness	**Nehemiah** Life-giving community and institutions
Mercy	Fulfillment	Self-gratification	Stubbornness	Pleasing God, not man	**Ammonite** Barrenness	Inability or failure to accept God's view & his love of you.	**John** God helping you possess your birthright

Transformative
Resources

Website

Transformation = www.TransformationBook.online

Books

Designed for Fulfillment, Charles R. Wale

Ekklesia, Ed Silvoso

LifeLift, Andrew Edwin Jenkins

Prayer Evangelism, Ed Silvoso

A Time to Advance, Chuck Pierce with Robert and Linda Heidler

A Time to Prosper, Chuck Pierce with Robert and Linda Heidler

Overview

On the following pages you'll find an outline of the material presented in this manual. This is placed here for quick review of the concepts.

THE PATH

IDENTITY

DISCOVER WHO GOD UNIQUELY MADE ME TO BE

ALIGNMENT

REORDER MY MOST VALUABLE ASSETS

EMPOWERMENT

TAKE THE PRESENCE WITH ME IN EVERY AREA OF LIFE

ASSIGNMENT

BLESS THE PEOPLE GOD PLACES BEFORE ME

4. Assignment   125

IDENTITY

DISCOVER WHO GOD UNIQUELY MADE ME TO BE

ALIGNMENT

REORDER MY MOST VALUABLE ASSETS

ASSIGNMENT

BLESS THE PEOPLE GOD PLACES BEFORE ME

EMPOWERMENT

TAKE THE PRESENCE WITH ME IN EVERY AREA OF LIFE

Made in the USA
Middletown, DE
26 September 2022

11302045R00113